JESUS AND CHRISTIAN ORIGINS
OUTSIDE THE NEW TESTAMENT

Jesus and Christian Origins Outside the New Testament

by

F. F. BRUCE
D.D., F.B.A.
Rylands Professor of Biblical Criticism and Exegesis
University of Manchester

WILLIAM B. EERDMANS PUBLISHING COMPANY
Grand Rapids, Michigan

BT
297
.B74
1974

First published 1974 by Hodder and Stoughton, Ltd., London.
This American edition by special arrangement with Hodder and
Stoughton.

First printing, April 1974
Second printing, December 1974

Library of Congress Cataloging in Publication Data

Bruce, Frederick Fyvie, 1910-
Jesus and Christian origins outside the New Testament.

Bibliography: p. 205 - 206.
1. Jesus Christ — Biography — Sources.
2. Christianity — Origin. I. Title.
BT297.B74   1974   232   74-2012
ISBN 0-8028-1575-8

To

Ward and Laurel Gasque

Publisher's Note

The aim of the continuing British series "Knowing Christianity," edited by William Neil and published by Hodder & Stoughton in London, is to provide for thinking laymen a solid but nontechnical presentation of what the Christian religion is and what it has to say. This new book by the renowned evangelical scholar F. F. Bruce — the fifteenth in the series — meets that objective admirably; and we are pleased to introduce it to American readers.

The question Professor Bruce answers here is a familiar one: What can we find out about Jesus Christ as an historical person outside of the New Testament? The contemporary evidence he considers comes from Qumran, Jewish, pagan, apocryphal, Islamic, and Gnostic documents as well as from archaeology. Professor Bruce emphasizes that he is not trying to prove from these secondary accounts the historicity of Jesus: that is the undertaking of students of the primary sources — the New Testament writings themselves. (He himself stands in the forefront of that number, of course, on the strength of numerous published writings on the subject, both technical and popular.) However, he stresses, the proliferation of legends about Jesus, the most important of which are discussed in this book, in no way witnesses against the historical validity of his life and mission; indeed, it attests rather to his increasing impact even among those who had no experience of his redeeming grace.

We commend this book as an enriching, fascinating, and helpful introduction to an area in the study of Christianity that is little known to many Christians.

Author's Preface

As we go (say) to the Qumran texts for first-hand testimony about the Qumran community, or to the Qur'ān for first-hand evidence on the rise of Islam, so we go to the New Testament writings for first-hand information about the origins of Christianity. In the other books which I have written on Christian origins, the New Testament writings have always provided the primary source material. Such information as we can glean from other sources is secondary in comparison with what they provide. But it is interesting to consider what other sources have to say, and the relevant material found in the most important of them is set out and discussed in this book.

I am indebted to Dr. William Neil, General Editor of 'Knowing Christianity', for the invitation to contribute this volume to the series, and to Miss Margaret Hogg for the almost incredible skill and patience with which, chapter by chapter, she transformed an untidy manuscript into a beautiful typescript.

F. F. B.

Contents

Abbreviations

CD	*Covenant of Damascus*, otherwise *Zadokite Work*
CIL	*Corpus Inscriptionum Latinarum* (Berlin)
CPI	*Corpus Papyrorum Iudaicarum* (ed. V. Tcherikover and A. Fuks)
Hist. Eccl.	*Ecclesiastical History* (Eusebius)
P. Lond.	*London Papyri* (British Museum)
P. Oxy.	*Oxyrhynchus Papyri*
P. Ryl.	Rylands Library Papyri (Manchester)
1QS	*Rule of the Community* from Qumran Cave 1
1QSb	*Blessings* from Qumran Cave 1
TB	Baylonian Talmud
TJ	Jerusalem (or Palestinian) Talmud

Introduction

SEVERAL years ago I received a letter propounding a question
of a kind which I am frequently asked to answer. The writer
was a Christian, to whom the question had been put by an
agnostic friend in the course of a lengthy discussion, and it had
caused him, he said, 'great concern and some little upset in my
spiritual life'.

Here is the question, as framed by my correspondent:

> What collateral proof is there in existence of the historical
> fact of the life of Jesus Christ? If the Bible account of his
> activities is accurate, he should have caused sufficient
> interest to gain considerable comment in other histories and
> records of the time; but in fact (I am told), apart from obscure
> references in Josephus and the like, no mention is made.
> The substantiation of the Gospels one from another is hardly
> acceptable, as it is internal, and such evidence would be
> inadmissible in any other form of enquiry. It is complicated,
> too, by the fact that the canon of Scripture was not compiled
> until many years after it was written, and then the decision
> of what was included or rejected was man-made. Is such
> collateral proof available, and if not, are there reasons for the
> lack of it?

Some parts of this question can be dismissed fairly briefly for
our present purpose, because they rest on misconceptions
which, however widely they may be entertained, can be easily
dispelled. This is so, for example, with his reference to the
canon of Scripture. Certainly the individual New Testament
documents were in existence some time before they were
gathered together in a canon (a list of authoritative documents).
As for the 'man-made' decision about their inclusion in such a
canon, or rejection from it, it must be remembered that there
was nothing arbitrary about this 'decision', nor was it a sudden,
once-for-all matter. The first time that a church council

promulgated a statement about which books made up the New Testament canon was in A.D. 393, and that council was merely a provincial synod in North Africa. It perpetrated no innovation, but simply recognised the situation which had been established by Christian use and wont over the preceding two hundred years and more. Inclusion in a canon conferred on no book an authority which it did not already possess; the books were included in the canon because of the authority accorded to them individually throughout the Christian world from the end of the first Christian century onwards. The issue of the canon is irrelevant to the general question put by my correspondent: it is with the separate documents as originally composed, and not with their subsequent inclusion in a sacred collection, that a historical enquiry is concerned.

A misconception of another kind underlies the statement that 'the substantiation of the Gospels one from another is hardly acceptable, as it is internal, and such evidence would be inadmissible in any other form of enquiry'. Just why would 'such evidence' be 'inadmissible in any other form of enquiry'? If we were dealing with four witnesses who had met together in advance and agreed on the story they were to tell, that might be a reasonable objection; but is it seriously suggested that the evidence of the four Gospel-writers is of this sort?

When my correspondent says that their evidence is 'internal', it is not quite clear what he means. He may mean that it is internal to the New Testament; but it is necessary to deal with the documents as they existed *before* there was a New Testament collection. He may mean, on the other hand, that their evidence is internal to the Christian movement, in the sense that it comes from within the church. That is so, but why should that reduce the value of their evidence? It is only natural that men who were closely associated with the movement should be more interested in writing about its Founder than outsiders would be.

It would be odd if anyone dismissed John Morley's *Life of Gladstone*[1] as worthless for factual information because the author was Gladstone's friend, political ally and cabinet colleague. The historian will know how to make the appropriate allowances for Morley's sympathies and perspective, but will acknowledge that the picture of Gladstone, as seen through the

[1] London: Macmillan (1903).

14

eyes of an associate who appreciated many — but not all! — of the
facets of Gladstone's personality, provides him with source
material of rare value. Nor would any historian ignore Sir
Winston Churchill's *The Second World War*[2] or Mr.
Harold Wilson's 'personal record' of *The Labour Government, 1964–
1970*,[3] on the ground that the authors occupied the position of
Prime Minister during the periods covered respectively by
these works and would therefore present biassed accounts. He
would easily make allowances for the authors' interested view-
points, but would readily acknowledge that an 'inside' account
is marked by valuable qualities of its own which could not be
matched in the most objective appraisal by an outsider.

No one supposes that the evangelists and other New Testament writers were dispassionate recorders, transmitting material
the truth or falsehood of which made no personal difference to
themselves. They were deeply committed men, writing not
merely to provide information but to commend their Saviour
to others. They make no attempt to conceal their interest and
aim, and the historian will take all this into his reckoning, while
acknowledging that they provide him with historical data the
like of which he could not find elsewhere.

In fact, no body of literature has been subjected, over the
past two centuries, to more intensive and critical analysis than
the New Testament writings in general and the four Gospels in
particular. It is on the basis of such scientific enquiry, not in
despite of it, that such a credible account of Jesus as that given
(say) by Professor C. H. Dodd in *The Founder of Christianity*[4]
is constructed. It was an odd aberration on the part of a distinguished modern historian when, reviewing Professor Dodd's
book, he depreciated the value of its sources (mainly the four
Gospels, with some contributions from other New Testament
documents) by observing that they survived in manuscripts not
earlier than the fourth century A.D. An odd aberration in two
respects: first, a gap of many more than three centuries between
the date of composition and the date of the earliest extant
manuscripts is nowhere reckoned to diminish the credibility
of the great classical historians (Herodotus, Thucydides and

---

[2] London: Cassell (1948–53).
[3] London: Weidenfeld and Nicolson (1972).
[4] London: Collins (Fontana Books, 1972).

Tacitus, for example); second, our oldest surviving manuscripts of the Gospels and the letters of Paul go back to the second century, not the fourth. As for the principal New Testament documents themselves, they belong to the first century. The Gospel of John is so well attested in the earlier part of the second century that it cannot be later than its traditional date, between A.D. 90 and 100 (nowadays some would date it earlier on the strength of its affinities with the Qumran texts). The three other Gospels and the Acts of the Apostles are earlier than John; and the letters of Paul are earlier still.

To suggest that the evidence of all the New Testament writers should be lumped together and allowed one point only, while non-Christian writers should be allowed one point each, would appear to be putting the former at an unfair disadvantage. Yet, it must be added, even if such an inequitable condition were insisted on for our enquiry, we should enter the debate quite cheerfully.

Examination of the New Testament writings, however, is not a subject of this book; I undertook that exercise a number of years ago in *The New Testament Documents . Are They Reliable?*[5] What we are looking at here is material outside the New Testament, what my correspondent calls 'collateral' testimony — references to Jesus and Christian origins in other texts, of the first and subsequent centuries, largely, but not exclusively, non-Christian.

Not all of the material in the following chapters provides the same kind of evidence. Much of it (such as that found in the Apocryphal Gospels and Islamic tradition) provides no historical evidence at all for Jesus and his first followers, but only for what was thought or imagined about them in later generations and centuries, and most of it presupposes some knowledge, or at least a dim memory, of the narratives in the four Gospels. The brief references in early Gentile writers are independent of the New Testament and of Christian influence; so are those in the authentic text of Josephus. The additions in the Slavonic Josephus, on the other hand, show clear signs of Christian authorship. Many of the rabbinical allusions reflect controversies between Jews and Jewish Christians. The Qumran manuscripts present evidence which is certainly independent of

[5] London: Inter-Varsity Press (5th edition, 1960).

Christianity, but since it is almost entirely pre-Christian evidence it is only background evidence. More background evidence, contemporary in date with the New Testament story, is provided by various forms of archaeological material. Some of the sayings ascribed to Jesus in the *Gospel of Thomas* and elsewhere, which are not paralleled in the New Testament, may be based on sound oral tradition, but each of them must be adjudged on its own merits.

When we are asked what 'collateral proof' exists of the life of Jesus Christ, would it be unfair to begin by asking another question? In which contemporary writers — in which writers who flourished, say, during the first fifty years after the death of Christ — would you expect to find the collateral evidence you are looking for? Well, perhaps it *would* be rather unfair, as the man in the street can hardly be expected to know who was writing in the Graeco-Roman world during those fifty years; the classical student himself has to scratch his head in an attempt to remember who they were. For it is surprising how few writings, comparatively speaking, have survived from those years of a kind which might be even remotely expected to mention Christ. (I except, for the present, the letters of Paul and several other New Testament writings.)

But let me word my question a little differently. In what *kind* of documents, during the first fifty years after the death of Christ, would you expect to find his name mentioned?

Perhaps a recent parallel will help us to answer that question. The *Illustrated London News* of April 30, 1960, carried a brief report (with photograph) of the death of one Hajji Mirza Ali Khan. In the closing years of the British Raj in India he was a militant opponent of British control of the Waziristan sector of the North-West Frontier. He figured in the press from time to time under the title 'the Fakir of Ipi'; but I do not suppose that he will play a prominent part in histories of the twentieth century.

Since the Fakir of Ipi was a holy man, I imagine that there was some religious basis for his activities, and I have no doubt that he had some devotees who thought him a very important person indeed. But if his devotees had suddenly begun to propagate a cult in which he played a central part; if their mission had proved unexpectedly successful; if it had led to riots in Karachi and Delhi; if it had been carried to London and had begun to cause trouble in the Indian or Pakistani communities here—then the name of the Fakir of Ipi would certainly have become familiar and would have found its way into historical writings. But such a process would take a little time.

May I suggest that in A.D. 30 the activity of Jesus of Nazareth would have meant no more to people living at the heart of the Roman world than the activity of the Fakir of Ipi meant to people in England? A religious leader who won a following by his claims to be a king, and who was conveniently executed—why, there were scores of people like that in Palestine in those days. Tiberius was emperor at the time but, as was pointed out at the beginning of an earlier volume in this series, a Roman historian who was not unaware of the circumstances of Jesus's execution can report with regard to Palestine: 'under Tiberius all quiet'.[6] When Jesus's followers, however, claiming that he had risen from the dead, began to proclaim him as the deliverer for whom the world was waiting, when their mission met with astonishing success, when it was carried not only to Antioch and Alexandria but to Rome itself, and led to riots there—then the name of Christ and of his followers, the Christians, became familiar at the heart of the Roman Empire. But, of course, that took a little time. And, while Christ and the Christians ultimately came to be mentioned in historical literature, the first Roman literature in which we might expect to find mention of them would be the police news. And that, in fact, is what we do find.

[6] W. H. C. Frend, *The Early Church* (London, 1965), p. 13, quoting Tacitus, *Histories* v. 9. Cf. p. 22.

Chapter One

The Evidence of Pagan Writers

PEOPLE frequently ask if any record has been preserved of the report which, it is presumed, Pontius Pilate, prefect of Judaea, sent to Rome concerning the trial and execution of Jesus of Nazareth. The answer is, none. But let it be added at once that no official record has been preserved of any report which Pontius Pilate, or any other Roman governor of Judaea, sent to Rome about anything. And only rarely has an official report from any governor of any Roman province survived. They may have sent in their reports regularly, but for the most part these reports were ephemeral documents, and in due course they disappeared.

In the early Christian centuries, Christian writers took it for granted that Pilate's report was filed somewhere in the imperial archives, and that it could be consulted by those who had access to these archives. Thus Justin Martyr, who wrote his *Defence of Christianity* about A.D. 150 and addressed it to the Emperor Antoninus Pius, was quite sure that the Christian account of the public life and death of Jesus could be verified by reference to the official records (the *acta*) of Pilate's term of office. Quoting Psalm 22. 16, he says:

> But the words, 'They pierced my hands and feet', refer to the nails which were fixed in Jesus's hands and feet on the cross; and after he was crucified, his executioners cast lots for his garments, and divided them among themselves. That these things happened you may learn from the 'Acts' which were recorded under Pontius Pilate.[1]

Later he says:

[1] Justin, *First Apology* 35. 7–9.

That he performed these miracles you may easily satisfy yourself from the 'Acts' of Pontius Pilate.[2]

Similarly both Justin and Tertullian, another Christian apologist of a generation or two later, were sure that the census which was held about the time of our Lord's birth was recorded in the official archives of the reign of Augustus, and that anyone who took the trouble to look these archives up would find the registration of Joseph and Mary there.[3]

Whether any of their readers did take the trouble to consult the records we cannot say. At a later date, possibly when the actual documents were no longer available, forged 'Acts of Pilate' made their appearance, which purported to give the procurator's official account of the events. Some of these were intended as an attack on Christianity; others were written to defend it. Of the 'Acts of Pilate' which were intended to refute the Christian claims, the best known are those published in A.D. 311 by Maximinus II, one of the last pagan emperors, which gave an unfavourable account of the life of Jesus and were recommended for reading and memorising in grammar schools. They were marred by historical errors—dating Jesus's death, for example, in A.D. 20.[4]

Of those which were composed by Christians, the best-known example is one that has come down under the alternative title of the *Gospel of Nicodemus* (at which we shall look later).[5]

In the absence of any authentic report of this kind, we move on to the next occasion when Christianity attracted the notice of the custodians of Roman law and order.

Suetonius and the Expulsion of Jews

In A.D. 49 a wave of riots broke out in the very large Jewish community in Rome. The trouble proved so intractable that the Emperor Claudius took the drastic step of banishing all Jews from the city. Among the ancient writers who mention this incident is Luke, who tells us in Acts 18. 2 that when Paul arrived in Corinth (*c.* A.D. 50) he found there 'a Jew named

[2] Justin, *First Apology* 48. 3.
[3] Justin, *First Apology* 34. 2; Tertullian, *Against Marcion* iv. 7, 19.
[4] Cf. Eusebius, *Hist. Eccl.* i. 9. 3 f.
[5] See p. 94.

Aquila, a native of Pontus, lately come from Italy with his wife Priscilla, because Claudius had commanded all the Jews to leave Rome'. One writer adds an interesting piece of information. This is the Roman author Suetonius, who about A.D. 120 compiled biographies of the first twelve Roman emperors, from Julius Caesar onward. In his *Life of Claudius* he says of that emperor:

> He expelled the Jews from Rome, on account of the riots in which they were constantly indulging, at the instigation of Chrestus.[6]

'Chrestus', a common slave-name, was a popular mis-spelling of the name of Christ. The situation referred to was probably the result of the recent introduction of Christianity into the Jewish community of Rome, with the controversy and quarrelling to which it gave rise. Police action was called for, and when, several decades later, a historian had occasion to mention the incident, the police records provided one of his sources of information. Only, the historian appears to have misunderstood the reference to one 'Chrestus' in the police records; he took the reference to mean that this 'Chrestus' was actually in Rome as ringleader of the riotous behaviour in A.D. 49, but it was in another way that 'Chrestus' became the occasion of these disorders.

The expulsion of the Jewish community from Rome caused a set-back to the progress of Christianity in that city, for in A.D. 49 it appears to have been only as a distinctive movement with Judaism that Christianity was known there. But with the death of Claudius in A.D. 54 the expulsion edict became a dead letter. Rome was soon as full of Jews as ever it had been, and the Christian cause was re-established there more securely than before, counting many Gentiles now among its adherents as well as Jews. Ten years later, Christianity figured again in the police news of the capital, this time in a more macabre fashion than on the previous occasion.

Tacitus and the Fire of Rome

In A.D. 64 a disastrous fire swept the city. Almost before the

[6] Suetonius, *Claudius* 25. 4. See also pp. 196 ff.

flames were beaten out, a rumour began to circulate that the fire was no accident — that it had been started and fostered by command of the Emperor Nero (stepson and successor to Claudius). Perhaps the rumour was ill-founded, but Nero judged that the best way to get rid of the odium that it bade fair to bring upon him was to divert the blame to someone else. So he arranged that the Christians of Rome should be charged with fire-raising, and many of them in consequence were burned on stakes or exposed to wild beasts. They were so unpopular that he thought they could be attacked with impunity.

Suetonius devotes a brief mention to this attack on the Christians of Rome in his *Life of Nero*, as he did to the expulsion of the Jews in his *Life of Claudius*:

> Punishment was inflicted on the Christians, a body of people addicted to a novel and mischievous superstition.[7]

But a fuller account of the matter is given by a contemporary of Suetonius, the Roman historian Tacitus. In the course of his *Roman Annals* (written between A.D. 115 and 117) Tacitus mentions the fire of Rome and Nero's attempt to fasten the blame on the Christians — 'a class of men loathed for their vices', he calls them. This is the first time that he has occasion to mention them, and so he gives a brief account of their origin:

> They got their name from Christ, who was executed by sentence of the procurator Pontius Pilate in the reign of Tiberius. That checked the pernicious superstition for a short time, but it broke out afresh — not only in Judaea, where the plague first arose, but in Rome itself, where all the horrible and shameful things in the world collect and find a home.[8]

When police news becomes sufficiently significant it provides the material for history, and this is illustrated in our passage from Tacitus. Not only was the action of the imperial police against the Christians of Rome worth recording (the more so in view of the dimensions to which Christianity had grown by the reign of Trajan, in which Tacitus was writing), but the

[7] Suetonius, *Nero* 16. 2.
[8] Tacitus, *Annals* xv. 44.

police action which had been carried out over thirty years previously, when Pilate was governor of Judaea, acquired a significance which no Roman could have foreseen in A.D. 30.

Pilate's execution of Christ, and any report that he may have sent to Rome about it, would never have been heard of again, if in fact that execution had put an end to the movement which Christ began. But when that movement, far from being crushed, advanced to Rome and attracted imperial attention there, there was some reason for investigating its origins. This Tacitus appears to have done. From the contemptuous and hostile tone which he adopts towards the Christians, we may gather that he did not seek his information from them. But if he did not seek it from them, where did he go for it? To some official record, perhaps—possibly to Pilate's report; who knows? Tacitus had an official standing which would give him access to such archives, if indeed they survived to his day.

Pilate is not mentioned in any other pagan document which has come down to us. (The character of the man and his governorship is tellingly described by the Jewish writers Philo and Josephus.)[9] And it may be regarded as an instance of the irony of history that the only surviving reference to him in a pagan writer mentions him because of the sentence of death which he passed upon Christ. For a moment Tacitus joins hands with the ancient Christian creed: '. . . suffered under Pontius Pilate'.

Pliny and Bithynian Christianity

Not only may police news provide the material for history, when it becomes sufficiently significant; it may also provide— in however incidental a fashion—the material for literature.

Tacitus and Suetonius had a contemporary called Pliny, who has established for himself a niche in posterity's memory by the way in which he acquitted himself as a man of letters. We may, indeed, call him a man of letters in two senses: first, in the general sense of his being a literary figure; second, in the sense that the particular *genre* of literature in which he distinguished himself was letter-writing.

[9] Philo, *Legation to Gaius* 299–305 (quoting a letter to the Emperor Gaius from Herod Agrippa I); Josephus, *War* ii. 169–77; *Antiquities* xviii. 55–64, 85–89.

Pliny is one of the world's great letter-writers, whose letters, unlike the ephemeral notes which most of us write, intended only for the perusal of the recipient, were written with one eye on a wider public and have attained the status of literary classics.

Pliny is usually called Pliny the Younger, to distinguish him from his uncle, Pliny the Elder, whose great work on *Natural History* is also a literary classic. The elder Pliny lost his life in the eruption of Vesuvius in A.D. 79, because his insatiable curiosity about the workings of nature brought him too close to the centre of volcanic activity.

In all, ten books of the younger Pliny's correspondence have come down to us. Of these the tenth has a special interest for us, because it contains his correspondence with the Emperor Trajan (A.D. 98–117). About A.D. 111 Pliny was appointed imperial legate of the Roman province of Bithynia, in north-west Asia Minor. During his period of office there, he conducted an assiduous correspondence with the emperor, consulting him on every point which called for a decision. Pliny shows himself, in fact, as the complete civil servant of caricature, incapable of taking any decision on his own initiative.

Pliny's letters to the emperor are rather wordy; the emperor's replies are terse and to the point. When, for example, there were one or two serious outbreaks of fire in the chief cities of the province, one might have expected the governor to take the appropriate steps in this matter at least on his own responsibility. But no; before organising a fire-brigade, he must consult the emperor.[10] And on this occasion the emperor's reply may surprise us:

Fire-brigades should not be organised. The proper course is for each property-owner and householder to have fire-fighting equipment constantly available, so that fires can be tackled before they spread too far. The trouble with fire-brigades is simply this: any organisation which brings men together, whatever its original and ostensible purpose may be, sooner or later develops into a secret society with subversive political aims.[11]

[10] Pliny, *Epistles* x. 33.
[11] Pliny, *Epistles* x. 34.

We may be surprised at the emperor's decision, but it was based on the experience of several generations of Roman political life. And it may help to explain in part the objection raised by enlightened administrators to meetings of Christians, whose claim to be a religious community was not admitted by imperial law.

How, in fact, enlightened administrators at this time viewed Christianity may be seen by another exchange of letters between Pliny and the emperor. Pliny, who had never had any official contact with Christians during the fifty years of his life thus far, found himself obliged to deal with them in Bithynia because of the rapidity with which they were spreading in the province. Inevitably, he consulted the emperor. And, just because Pliny's letters had the salt of literary immortality about them, what would normally have been a routine matter of administrative correspondence has been preserved to our day, and from it we derive information about a police action of which we should otherwise have known nothing.

Here, then, is Pliny's letter to Trajan on the subject:

My Lord: It is my custom to consult you whenever I am in doubt about any matter; who is better able to direct my hesitation or instruct my ignorance?

I have never been present at Christian trials; consequently I do not know the precedents regarding the question of punishment or the nature of the inquisition. I have been in no little doubt whether some discrimination is made with regard to age, or whether the young are treated no differently from the older; whether renunciation wins indulgence, or it is of no avail to have abandoned Christianity if one has once been a Christian; whether the very profession of the name is to be punished, or only the disgraceful practices which go along with the name.

So far this has been my procedure when people were charged before me with being Christians. I have asked the accused themselves if they were Christians; if they said 'Yes', I asked them a second and third time, warning them of the penalty; if they persisted I ordered them to be led off to execution. For I had no doubt that, whatever kind of thing it was that they pleaded guilty to, their stubbornness and unyielding obstinacy at any rate deserved to be punished. There were others afflicted with the like madness whom I marked down to be referred to Rome, because they were Roman citizens.

Later, as usually happens, the trouble spread by the very fact that it was being dealt with, and further varieties came to my notice. An anonymous document was laid before me containing many people's names. Some of these denied that they were Christians or had ever been so; at my dictation they invoked the gods and did reverence with incense and wine to your image, which I had ordered to be brought for this purpose along with the statues of the gods; they also cursed Christ; and as I am informed that people who are really Christians cannot possibly be made to do any of those things, I considered that the people who did them should be discharged. Others against whom I received information said they were Christians and then denied it; they meant (they said) that they had once been Christians but had given it up: some three years previously, some a longer time, one or two as many as twenty years before. All these likewise did reverence to your image and the statues of the gods and cursed Christ. But they maintained that their fault or error amounted to nothing more than this: they were in the habit of meeting on a certain fixed day before sunrise and reciting an antiphonal hymn to Christ as God, and binding themselves with an oath — not to commit any crime, but to abstain from all acts of theft, robbery and adultery, from breaches of faith, from repudiating a trust when called upon to honour it. After this, they went on, it was their custom to separate, and then meet again to partake of food, but food of an ordinary and innocent kind. And even this, they said, they had given up doing since the publication of my edict in which, according to your instructions, I had placed a ban on private associations. So I thought it the more necessary to inquire into the real truth of the matter by subjecting to torture two female slaves, who were called 'deacons'; but I found nothing more than a perverse superstition which went beyond all bounds.

Therefore I deferred further inquiry in order to apply to you for a ruling. The case seemed to me to be a proper one for consultation, particularly because of the number of those who were accused. For many of every age, every class, and of both sexes are being accused and will continue to be accused. Nor has this contagious superstition spread through the cities only, but also through the villages and the countryside. But I think it can be checked and put right. At any rate the temples, which had been wellnigh abandoned, are beginning to be frequented again; and the customary services, which had been neglected for a long time, are beginning to be resumed; fodder for the sacrificial animals, too, is beginning to find a sale again, for hitherto it was difficult to find anyone to buy it. From all this it is easy to judge what a multitude of people can be reclaimed, if an opportunity is granted them to renounce Christianity.[12]

And here is Trajan's reply:

My dear Secundus:[13] You have acted with perfect correctness in deciding the cases of those who have been charged before you with being Christians. Indeed, no general decision can be made by which a set form of dealing with them could be established. They must not be ferreted out; if they are charged and convicted, they must be punished, provided that anyone who denies that he is a Christian and gives practical proof of that by invoking our gods is to be pardoned on the strength of this repudiation, no matter what grounds for suspicion may have existed against him in the past. Anonymous documents which are laid before you should receive no attention in any case; they form a very bad precedent and are quite unworthy of the age in which we live.[14]

The correspondence between Pliny and Trajan about the Christian problem presents many features of interest. One such feature is the evident rapid increase of Christianity in Bithynia and Pontus.

We know from the First Epistle of Peter that there were Christians in these provinces in New Testament times, for they

---

[12] Pliny, *Epistles* x. 96.
[13] Pliny's full name was Gaius Plinius Secundus; Trajan addresses him here by his *cognomen* Secundus.
[14] Pliny, *Epistles* x. 97.

were among the people to whom that letter was addressed.[15] But by the time of Pliny's governorship they had grown so numerous that the pagan temples were being neglected and the purveyors of fodder for the sacrificial animals found their livelihood threatened. It may well have been these purveyors and others in a similar situation who drew the governor's attention to the growing menace of Christianity. With them we may compare the guild of silversmiths at Ephesus in Paul's day, who were so alarmed when they realised that the devotees of Great Artemis would no longer buy miniature silver shrines of the goddess if they became Christians.[16]

In the second place, Pliny's account of Christian practice has a special interest, and corroborates in general what we can glean from other quarters about Christian worship at this time. The evidence of the female 'deacons' may have been given under torture—they were slaves, and Roman magistrates did not attach any value to the evidence of slaves unless it was given under torture—but their evidence was true. The claim that they abjured all vicious or criminal acts, and that the food eaten in their meetings was 'food of an ordinary and innocent kind', was no doubt intended to rebut the charges of incendiarism, incest and ritual cannibalism which were popularly circulated against the Christians.

Two separate meetings are mentioned—one 'on a certain fixed day before sunrise' (i.e. early on Sunday morning) at which they sang an anthem ascribing divine honours to Christ and perhaps observed the Holy Communion, and one later in the day when they held an *agapē* or fellowship-meal. The 'oath' which they are said to have sworn at the earlier meeting is called a *sacramentum* in Pliny's Latin, and the word probably includes something like the sense which we attach to the term 'sacrament'.[17]

A third point of interest is the refusal of the Christians to venerate the images of pagan deities or to pay divine honours to the emperor. In accounts of the trials of Christians which have come down to us from the early centuries of our era this

[15] 1 Peter 1. 1.
[16] Acts 19. 24–27.
[17] The commonest use of *sacramentum* in classical Latin is for the oath of military obedience sworn by Roman soldiers on enlistment.

refusal regularly appears as the crucial test. Humane and reasonable magistrates might acknowledge that Christians were innocent of the crimes vulgarly alleged against them; they might even concede their right to follow their own religion, superstitious though they thought it. But there was a well-established way in which people whose loyalty was suspect might remove that suspicion: they might carry out a formal act of homage to the state gods and to the imperial image. If they refused to do this, the suspicion of disloyalty was confirmed, and they had to take the consequences.

For Christians such acts were idolatrous, and a verbal acknowledgment of the emperor's divinity was high treason to Christ, their only divine Lord. If their protestations of loyalty were not believed unless they consented to do things which (as Pliny was informed) 'people who are really Christians cannot possibly be made to do', then they were prepared to suffer.

And fourthly, it is striking that the emperor cites no statute or precedent to guide Pliny in his perplexity. Christianity had not yet been named explicitly as an offence on the Roman statute-book. Pliny asks whether it is the profession of the Christian name that is criminal, or only 'the disgraceful practices which go along with the name', but the emperor does not tell him.

Thus far Christianity was simply a matter for summary police action. Trajan's advice, too, is noteworthy: the Christians, he said, were not to be ferreted out, but if they came under the observation of the proconsular court and were convicted, they had to be punished. Christian apologists might cry out against the inconsistency of this ruling—'he says they must not be ferreted out, as though they were innocent', Tertullian later complains; 'he orders them to be punished, as though they were guilty!'[18]—but Trajan himself no doubt thought that his ruling was the most statesmanlike course in the circumstances. Christianity, he thought, was dangerous, but not frightfully dangerous.

Thallus and the Passion Narrative

There is some reason to believe that Christianity found literary mention at Rome many years before Tacitus or

[18] Tertullian, *Apology* 2. 8.

Suetonius or Pliny wrote. About A.D. 52 a writer named Thallus —thought by some to be a Samaritan by birth, who had been a freedman of the Emperor Tiberius[19]—wrote a history of the Eastern Mediterranean world from the Trojan War down to his own day. This history has unfortunately disappeared, but it was known to a Christian writer on chronology, Julius Africanus, who lived in the early part of the third century.

Julius Africanus describes the earthquake and the preternatural darkness which accompanied the crucifixion of Christ, and says that Thallus, in his third book, explained this darkness as an eclipse of the sun. (He also points out that Thallus's explanation was unacceptable, because Jesus was crucified at full moon, when no eclipse of the sun is possible.)[20] We may wish that we had the actual passage from Thallus to compare with Julius Africanus's account; but it is a reasonable inference that Thallus knew the Christian narrative of the crucifixion of Christ, and made some reference to it in his work.

The riots which led to the expulsion of Jews from Rome a few years before meant that some knowledge of Christianity was available in that city around the time when Thallus was writing. And not many years later the arrival of Paul in Rome to have his appeal heard before the imperial tribunal meant that some official quarters there were obliged to take more serious cognizance of Christianity. It may have been in part to supply the necessary information to such official quarters (of which Theophilus would be a representative) that Paul's friend Luke wrote his history of Christian origins—or rather the first draft of it.

Mara bar Serapion

A Syriac manuscript in the British Museum preserves the text of a letter written some indeterminate time later than A.D. 73 by a man named Mara bar Serapion to his son Serapion. Mara bar Serapion was in prison at the time, but he wrote to encourage his son in the pursuit of wisdom, and pointed out that those who persecuted wise men were overtaken by mis-

[19] This depends on his doubtful identification with a wealthy Samaritan freedman of Tiberius who, according to Josephus (*Antiquities* xviii. 167), lent a large sum of money to Herod Agrippa I.

[20] The quotation from Julius Africanus is accessible in F. Jacoby, *Die Fragmente der griechischen Historiker* II B (Berlin, 1929), p. 1157.

fortune. He instances the deaths of Socrates, Pythagoras and Christ:

> What advantage did the Athenians gain from putting Socrates to death? Famine and plague came upon them as a judgment for their crime. What advantage did the men of Samos gain from burning Pythagoras? In a moment their land was covered with sand. What advantage did the Jews gain from executing their wise King? It was just after that that their kingdom was abolished. God justly avenged these three wise men: the Athenians died of hunger; the Samians were overwhelmed by the sea; the Jews, ruined and driven from their land, live in complete dispersion. But Socrates did not die for good; he lived on in the teaching of Plato. Pythagoras did not die for good; he lived on in the statue of Hera. Nor did the wise King die for good; he lived on in the teaching which he had given.[21]

This writer can scarcely have been a Christian, or he would have said that Christ lived on by being raised from the dead. He was more probably a Gentile philosopher, who led the way in what later became a commonplace — the placing of Christ on a comparable footing with the great sages of antiquity. That he was influenced by Christians is evident from the way in which he makes 'the Jews' (not the Romans) the executioners of 'their wise King' and sees in the aftermath of the Jewish revolt of A.D. 66–73 a divine judgment on them for his execution.

[21] British Museum Syriac MS. Additional 14,658. The date of the *manuscript* is seventh century; the letter itself is some centuries earlier (second or third century). The writer's historical information about Athens and Samos is very inaccurate.

Chapter Two

The Evidence of Josephus

HAVING reviewed references to Jesus and the early Christians in Gentile writers, we now turn to Jews of the early centuries A.D. and ask what contribution they make to our subject.

Of all the Jewish writings which call for our attention there is none to compete in interest or importance with those of Josephus. But in order to understand Josephus's point of view we should begin by saying something about the man himself.

Josephus was one of those people who are born with a good conceit of themselves, and never lose it. He was born about A.D. 37 into a distinguished priestly family of Judaea and, if we may accept his own account, was a precocious youth, making trial in turn of three out of the four leading religious sects of his nation – Sadducees, Essenes and Pharisees. His experience of the three decided him to adhere to the Pharisees. At the age of twenty-six he took part in a delegation to Rome, and there he was able to assess at first hand the strength of the Roman Empire. Nevertheless, when a national revolt against Rome broke out three years later – A.D. 66 – he took a prominent part in resisting the Romans and was appointed commander of the insurgent forces in Galilee.

When the resistance in Galilee was crushed in the summer of A.D. 67, Josephus was brought before Vespasian, the Roman general charged with suppressing the revolt, whom he told that one day he would become emperor. Vespasian was sufficiently impressed by this prediction to order Josephus's life to be spared; but kept him a prisoner to see if his prophecy would come true. When it did come true two years later, Josephus received his liberty.

More astonishing than Josephus's successful prediction is the process of argument which led him to it: he had just come to the conclusion that the ancient Hebrew oracles which foretold

32

the emergence of a world-ruler from Judaea pointed not to someone of Jewish stock but to the commander of the Roman armies
in Judaea. Among those oracles he probably had particularly in
mind the words of Jacob in Genesis 49. 10:

> The sceptre shall not depart from Judah,
>   nor the ruler's staff from between his feet,
> until he comes to whom it belongs;
>   and to him shall be the obedience of the peoples.

In other words, Vespasian was the promised Messiah.[1]

That a patriotic Jew could entertain such a perverted interpretation of Israel's ancestral hope may seem almost incredible,
and indeed we are indebted for our knowledge of the matter to
Josephus's own account, written down by him some time after
Vespasian's assumption of the imperial purple; but there is no
reason to doubt that in general his account of the matter is a
true one, although it may have been touched up here and there
in the light of later developments. It appears, too, that Josephus
was influenced by a calculation according to which Daniel's
'seventy weeks' or 490 years (Daniel 9. 24–27) were due to
expire around that time, and he probably identified Vespasian
with 'the prince who is to come' of Daniel 9. 26.[2]

Josephus's fellow-countrymen did not appreciate the
subtlety of his motives for going over to the enemy side, and
have tended to regard him ever since as a renegade and traitor.
Yet, according to his lights, however dim they were, Josephus
did what he believed to be the best thing for his nation, and
when the war was over he devoted the second half of his life,
which he spent in Rome as a pensioner of the imperial house,
to writing in defence of the prestige of the Jews with which his
own prestige was intimately bound up.

Naturally, Josephus would not write anything calculated to
offend his Roman patrons, especially during the reign of

---

[1] Josephus, *War* iii. 392–408.

[2] We have to account for the widespread belief, attested not only by
Josephus (*War* vi. 312 f.) but also by Tacitus (*History* v. 13) and Suetonius
(*Vespasian* 4), that the sacred writings of the Jews pointed to the emerging
of world-rule from Judaea 'at that very time'. There is no precise time-
indication in Genesis 49. 10, but Josephus points out elsewhere (*Antiquities*
x. 267) that Daniel, unlike the other Hebrew prophets, was enabled to point
to the time at which his predictions would be fulfilled.

Vespasian's second son Domitian (A.D. 81–96) — a man cursed with an insanely suspicious nature and also with an irrational anti-Jewish prejudice. This must be borne in mind when we consider his allusions to Christian beginnings. For these appear in his *Jewish Antiquities*, a long work of twenty books which was written towards the end of Domitian's reign. He wrote this work, covering the history of the Jewish nation from its remotest origins down to his own day, in order to show that the antiquity and record of the Jewish nation compared favourably with those of the most renowned of the Gentile nations.

Josephus and John the Baptist

In his eighteenth book of these *Antiquities* he mentions a severe defeat which Herod Antipas, tetrarch of Galilee, suffered at the hands of the king of the Nabataean Arabs.[3] The Arab king had good cause to be indignant with Herod, for he was the father of Herod's former wife whom he divorced in order to marry his own niece and sister-in-law Herodias. Josephus says:

Some of the Jews thought that the destruction of Herod's army was a divine judgment, a very just penalty for his murder of John the Baptist. For Herod killed him in spite of the fact that he was a good man, who taught the Jews to practise virtue, to show righteousness towards one another and piety towards God, and to form a community by means of baptism. This baptism, he taught, was acceptable to God if those who underwent it did so not to procure remission of sins but to purify the body after the soul had already been purified by righteousness. His fellow-Jews gathered round him, for they were greatly impressed when they heard him preach. But Herod was afraid that his great power of persuading men might lead to a rising, for the people seemed ready to follow his counsel in everything. So he thought it advisable to arrest him and kill him before he started a revolt; this, he thought, was better than to repent after the event, once a revolt had broken out. So John, falling a victim to Herod's suspicion, was sent in chains to the fortress of Machaerus . . . and put to death there. The Jews, then,

[3] The king was Aretas IV (9 B.C.–A.D. 40), mentioned by Paul in 2 Corinthians 11. 32.

believed that it was to avenge John that God brought this disaster upon Herod's army.[4]

Herod may well have had political reasons for imprisoning John, as Josephus suggests, over and above his annoyance at John's denunciation of his illicit marriage with Herodias. There is no real contradiction here with the account given by the Synoptic Evangelists. There is a clear contradiction, however, between Josephus's statement that John's baptism was not directed towards the remission of sins and the New Testament's affirmation that this was exactly what it was for. The discovery and study of the Dead Sea Scrolls, however, have shown us what has happened.

Josephus assumes that John's baptism was of the same character as Essene baptism. Essene baptism, or at any rate the baptism practised by the Qumran group of Essenes, was a ritual cleansing of the body to be undergone only by those whose souls were already purified by righteousness.[5] Josephus had experience of the Essenes, but of John's baptism he had only hearsay knowledge. But when Josephus speaks of John as forming a community 'by means of baptism' his language is in line with that of Luke 1. 17, where John comes 'to make ready for the Lord a people prepared'.

When we read the New Testament, we think of John the Baptist mainly as Jesus's forerunner. This, however, is a peculiarly Christian insight, and one which we need not expect Josephus to share. Christians rarely think of John except within the context of Christian beginnings, but Josephus does not place him in such a context or relate him in any way with Christianity.

Josephus and James the Just

We come closer to Christian beginnings with a passage in the twentieth book of the *Antiquities*, where Josephus mentions the death of another well-known religious leader. He tells how the Roman procurator Festus died suddenly in office (*c.* A.D. 62) and how an interregnum of three months elapsed before his successor Albinus arrived in Judaea.

---

[4] Josephus, *Antiquities* xviii. 116–19.
[5] This is evident from the Qumran *Rule of the Community* (1QS) 3. 2–8. (On the Qumran documents see p. 66 ff.)

Early in this interregnum a new high priest was appointed—Annas the younger, a son of that Annas who is mentioned in the Gospels of Luke (3. 2) and John (18. 13) and in Acts (4. 6). The younger Annas quickly seized the opportunity to pay off a number of old scores in the absence of a Roman governor. So, says Josephus:

> he convened a judicial session of the Sanhedrin and brought before it the brother of Jesus the so-called Christ—James by name—and some others, whom he charged with breaking the law and handed over to be stoned to death.[6]

For this excess of authority Annas, whom Josephus describes as extremely rash and ruthless, was immediately deprived of his high-priesthood.

This James was James the Just, whom we know from the New Testament records to have been leader of the church of Jerusalem.[7] Josephus's statement that he was 'the brother of Jesus the so-called Christ' agrees with Paul's description of him in Galatians 1. 19 as 'James, the Lord's brother'.

From the tradition of James's character and death which was preserved in the church of Jerusalem we know that he enjoyed the respect of the Jewish people, most of whom were horrified at the high priest's action against him: and, indeed, when the Jewish revolt against Rome broke out a few years later and ended with the destruction of the city and temple of Jerusalem there were not wanting those who said that this disaster had come about because the prayers of James were no longer available to avert it.

Here, then, we come rather nearer to our main subject, although Josephus, probably deliberately, avoids referring to James as a leader of the Christians. His identification of James as 'the brother of Jesus the so-called Christ' makes us ask if his works contain any more direct reference to Jesus. There is one such passage in the manuscript tradition of his works. We must now examine its authenticity and significance.

Josephus and Jesus

In the eighteenth book of his *Jewish Antiquities* Josephus gives

[6] Josephus, *Antiquities* xx. 200.
[7] Cf. Acts 15. 13; 21. 18; Galatians 2. 9, 12.

an account of various troubles that befell the people of Judaea during the governorship of Pontius Pilate (A.D. 26–36), and the text of this section, as it has been handed down to us, contains the following paragraph, which we quote first according to William Whiston's translation:[8]

> Now, there was about this time Jesus, a wise man, if it be lawful to call him a man, for he was a doer of wonderful works, a teacher of such men as receive the truth with pleasure. He drew over to him both many of the Jews, and many of the Gentiles. He was the Christ. And when Pilate, at the suggestion of the principal men amongst us, had condemned him to the cross, those that loved him at the first did not forsake him; for he appeared to them alive again at the third day; as the divine prophets had foretold these and ten thousand other wonderful things concerning him. And the tribe of Christians, so named from him, are not extinct at this day.[9]

We know from the writings of Eusebius, the fourth-century bishop of Caesarea, that this paragraph was present in the works of Josephus as he knew them, for he quotes it in his *Ecclesiastical History*, written about A.D. 325, and in his *Demonstration of the Gospel*, written somewhat earlier.[10] But if we look at it carefully, it contains some expressions which only a Christian could seriously use—and Josephus was certainly no Christian. For example, the clause 'if it be lawful to call him a man' looks like a safeguard inserted by some sensitively orthodox Christian to remind readers of the truth that Jesus was divine as well as human. The sentence 'He was the Christ' would be a straightforward confession of faith in Jesus as the Messiah, unless it simply means that this Jesus was the person commonly known among the Gentiles as 'Christ'. But we might have expected Josephus in that case to use the same sort of language as he does when he records the trial and execution of

---

[8] William Whiston (1667–1752), Sir Isaac Newton's successor in the Chair of Mathematics at Cambridge, published in 1736 what may be called the 'authorised' English version of *The Works of Josephus*.

[9] Josephus, *Antiquities* xviii. 63 f.

[10] Eusebius, *Hist. Eccl.* i. 11. 7 f.; *Demonstration* iii. 5. 105.

James the brother of Jesus; that is to say, we might have expected him to add the qualification 'so-called' before 'Christ'. Josephus did not believe that Jesus was the Messiah; as we have seen, he recognised the Messiah in the Roman Emperor Vespasian. Again, the references to the resurrection of Jesus in this paragraph would suggest that Josephus not only believed in it but held that it had been foretold (together with many other facts about Jesus) in the Old Testament writings.

The church father Origen, writing about a century earlier than Eusebius, knew Josephus's references to John the Baptist and James the brother of Jesus, but states that Josephus 'did not believe in Jesus as the Christ'.[11] Formally, this contradicts the statement in the paragraph quoted above that 'He was the Christ'; and many students have come to the conclusion that the paragraph was interpolated by some Christian copyist or editor into the record of Josephus between the time of Origen and the time of Eusebius. It is a reasonable conclusion, held by many Christian scholars; and we must not accuse a man of undermining the case for historic Christianity because he cannot accept the authenticity of this paragraph. For, after all, it is not on the authority of Josephus that Christians believe in Christ!

But a case can be made out for the view that the paragraph preserves a genuine reference to Christ by Josephus, which has, however, been subjected to modification by Christian scribes. The passage contains some characteristic samples of the diction of Josephus — perhaps one should say the diction of the literary 'ghost' whom he employed to turn his material into stylish Greek.

The late Professor Joseph Klausner, of the Hebrew University of Jerusalem, suggests that the paragraph, as originally written, ran like this:

Now, there was about this time Jesus, a wise man; for he was a doer of wonderful works, a teacher of such men as receive the truth with pleasure. He drew over to him both many of the Jews and many of the Gentiles. And when Pilate, at the suggestion of the principal men among us, had condemned him to the cross, those that loved him at the first ceased not

[11] Origen, *Against Celsus* i. 47; *Commentary on Matthew* x. 17.

so to do; and the race of Christians, so named from him, are not extinct even now.[12]

This attempt to reconstruct what Josephus originally wrote amounts simply to the extrusion of those words which are felt to be Christian interpolations. But if in fact the original text was tampered with, it is possible that the tampering was not restricted to interpolation; it may have included the removal or modification of expressions felt to be offensive. At the time when Josephus was writing his *Antiquities* (about A.D. 93), he had to be very cautious in what he said, for the Emperor Domitian, whose pensioner he was, was becoming increasingly suspicious of anything that savoured of sedition, and Jews and Christians were prominent objects of his suspicion. It is unlikely in any case that Josephus would express any favourable opinion of Christ and Christianity, and doubly unlikely in those circumstances.

It has been argued, in the light of the context in which the paragraph appeared, that something of this sort is what Josephus said:

Now there arose about this time *a source of further trouble* in one Jesus, a wise man who performed surprising works, a teacher of men who gladly welcome *strange things*. He led away many Jews, and also many of the Gentiles. He was the *so-called* Christ. When Pilate, acting on information supplied by the chief men among us, condemned him to the cross, those who had attached themselves to him at first did not cease *to cause trouble*, and the tribe of Christians, which has taken this name from him, is not extinct even today.

The flavour of this rendering probably expresses Josephus's intention more closely. It includes four emendations, which are italicised above. The first one, suggested by Robert Eisler,[13] is the addition of the phrase 'a source of further trouble' in the first sentence. This links the paragraph more naturally to what

[12] J. Klausner, *Jesus of Nazareth* (London, 1929), pp. 55 ff. A similar reconstruction was suggested by T. Reinach, 'Josèphe sur Jésus', *Revue des Études Juives* 35 (1897), pp. 13 f.

[13] R. Eisler, *The Messiah Jesus and John the Baptist* (London, 1931), pp. 50 f. See p. 45.

has gone before, for Josephus has been narrating various troubles which arose during Pilate's governorship. The second one, suggested by H. St. J. Thackeray, is the reading 'strange things' (Gk. *aēthē*) instead of 'true things' (Gk. *alēthē*).[14] To Josephus, Christianity was certainly more strange than true. The third one, suggested by G. C. Richards and R. J. H. Shutt, is the insertion of 'so-called' before 'Christ'.[15] This brings the expression into line with Josephus's language in his reference to James the Lord's brother. Some reference to our Lord's designation 'the Christ' is required at this point; otherwise Josephus's readers might not understand how in fact the 'tribe of Christians' got its name from Jesus. The fourth is not an emendation in the same sense as the others. Josephus says that Jesus's disciples 'did not cease', and we have to ask, 'did not cease to do what?' The answer will be in accordance with the context, and in the kind of context we envisage 'did not cease to cause trouble' makes good sense.[16]

Conjectural emendation is, at best, conjectural. But it seems clear (*a*) that Josephus's paragraph about Jesus is not a wholesale interpolation; (*b*) that Josephus did not write it in the form in which it has been handed down to us. If that is so, recourse must be had to conjectural emendation in an endeavour to reconstruct the passage as Josephus might have written it. But we may live in hope that one day a second-century fragment of Josephus's *Antiquities* will come to light, including this part of the work. In that event, our conjectural emendations may be dismissed, having served their purpose; but no doubt other problems will be raised to take the place of those which we try to solve at present by emendation.

It may be said, however, that Josephus bears witness to Jesus's date, to his being the brother of James the Just, to his reputation as a miracle-worker, to his crucifixion under Pilate as a consequence of charges brought against him by the Jewish

[14] H. St. J. Thackeray, *Josephus the Man and the Historian* (New York, 1929), pp. 144 f.

[15] G. C. Richards and R. J. H. Shutt, 'Critical Notes on Josephus' *Antiquities*', *Classical Quarterly* 31 (1937), p. 176; G. C. Richards, 'The *Testimonium* of Josephus', *Journal of Theological Studies* 42 (1941), pp. 70 f.

[16] Some scholars have held that the infinitive 'to cause trouble' actually appeared here in the original text of Josephus; cf. F. Scheidweiler, 'Sind die Interpolationen im altrussischen Josephus wertlos?', *Zeitschrift für die neutestamentliche Wissenschaft* 43 (1950–51), pp. 155 ff., especially pp. 176–8.

rulers, to his claim to be the Messiah, and to his being the founder of the 'tribe of Christians'.[17]

There is no further reference to Jesus or to the beginnings of Christianity in the Greek text of Josephus. But further references do occur in one version of his *History of the Jewish War*; and they must next claim our attention.

[17] A tenth-century Arabic version of Josephus's paragraph about Jesus, by a Syrian bishop named Agapius, has been published by S. Pines in *An Arabic Version of the Testimonium Flavianum and its Implications* (Israel Academy of Sciences and Humanities, Jerusalem, 1971). This version may preserve a less thorough-going Christian editing of the original than does the traditional Greek text; at any rate it helps to confirm that Josephus did write about Jesus.

Chapter Three

The Slavonic Josephus

THE first work to be composed by Josephus, when he went to Rome after A.D. 70 to spend the rest of his life there as a pensioner of the imperial house, was a *History of the Jewish War*. It is our chief source of information for the events leading up to the outbreak of the Jewish war with Rome in A.D. 66 and for the course of that war until the storming of the Jewish fortress of Masada in 73. One of the aims of this work is to show the irresistible might of Rome, and thus to warn others who might be tempted to rebel against her. It was published in two editions — first an Aramaic edition, for the benefit of the Jews of Mesopotamia, and later a Greek edition, for more general consumption. The Aramaic edition has not survived.

In the eleventh or twelfth century A.D. a Slavonic version of this work appeared — more precisely, an Old Russian version. It did not excite much interest in the western world until 1906, when several extracts from it were published in a German translation[1] — extracts which referred to John the Baptist and Jesus and to other persons and incidents mentioned in the New Testament.

These extracts do not appear in the Greek edition of the *History of the Jewish War* which has come down to us, but it has been suggested that they were derived, directly or indirectly, from the lost Aramaic edition.[2] This is not very likely; no traces of Semitic idiom have been detected in these additions. In fact, it is as certain as anything can be in the realm of literary criticism that they were not part of what Josephus wrote at all, but had been interpolated into the Greek manuscripts from which the Old Russian translation was made. Even as inter-

---

[1] A. Berendts, *Die Zeugnisse vom Christentum im slavischen 'De Bello Judaico' des Josephus — Texte und Untersuchungen* 29. 4 (Leipzig, 1906).

[2] There are other interpolations in the Old Russian edition over and above those which ostensibly bear on the beginnings of Christianity.

polations, some of them have an interest of their own, because they represent significant traditions; but they cannot be used as contemporary or even near-contemporary evidences for Christian beginnings.

References to Jesus

The most interesting, which purports to be an account of Jesus, is interpolated into the second book of the *Jewish War*, and its opening section is plainly an expanded version of the traditional text of the testimony to Jesus already quoted from the *Antiquities*. It runs as follows:

At that time there appeared a certain man — if it is proper to call him a man, for his nature and form were human, but his appearance was superhuman and his works were divine. It is therefore impossible for me to call him a mere man; but on the other hand, if I consider that his nature was shared by others, I will not call him an angel. Everything that he performed through an invisible power he wrought by word and command. Some said: 'Our first lawgiver is risen from the dead, and he has displayed signs and wonders'. But others thought that he was sent from God. In many respects, however, he opposed the law and he did not keep the sabbath according to the custom of our forefathers. Yet he did nothing shameful. He did nothing with his hands, but with his bare word alone. Many of the common people followed him and paid heed to his teaching. And many men's minds were stirred, for they thought that through him the Jewish tribes could free themselves from the power of Rome. It was his custom to stay outside the city on the Mount of Olives. There he wrought cures for the people. A hundred and fifty assistants joined him, and a multitude of the populace. When they saw his power, and his ability to accomplish by a word whatever he desired, they communicated to him their will that he should enter the city, cut down the Roman troops and Pilate, and reign over them; but he would not listen to them. When news of this was brought to the Jewish leaders, they assembled along with the high priest and said: 'We are too powerless and weak to resist the Romans. But since the bow is bent, we will go and tell Pilate what we have heard, and then we shall avoid trouble; for if he hears of it from others we shall be robbed of our goods and we shall be slaughtered and our children dispersed.' So they went and told Pilate. Pilate sent soldiers who killed many of the multitude.[3] The miracle-worker was brought before him, and after he held an inquiry concerning him, he pronounced judgment as follows: 'He is a benefactor, he is no criminal, no rebel, no seeker after kingship.' So he released him, for he had healed his wife when she was dying. He went back to his usual place and did his customary works. Even more people gathered round him, and he gained even more glory by his acts. The scribes were stung with envy, and they gave Pilate thirty talents to kill him. He took it and gave them liberty to carry out their will. So they seized him and crucified him, contrary to the law of their fathers.[4]

This account of events leading up to the death of Jesus deviates from the New Testament account very materially; yet it is definitely a Christian and not a Jewish account. For one thing, it reflects the increasing Christian tendency to whitewash Pontius Pilate, and put the responsibility for Jesus's death exclusively on the Jewish leaders, to the point where they are represented as actually carrying out the work of crucifixion themselves — a sheer historical impossibility.[5] The thirty silver shekels which, in Matthew's narrative (26. 15), the chief priests gave Judas Iscariot for betraying Jesus to them have been transformed into thirty talents (3,000 times as much) with which they are said to have bribed Pilate. The use of the Mount of Olives as a base from which to attack the Roman garrison in Jerusalem resembles Josephus's account of an Egyptian insurgent leader who planned such an attack about A.D. 54 (cf. Acts 21. 38).[6] The transference of the incident to Jesus may be based on the statement in John 6. 15 that, after the

[3] Cf. Luke 13. 1.

[4] Immediately after *War* ii. 174.

[5] The phrase 'contrary to the law of their fathers' implies that such a mode of execution was foreign to Jewish procedure. The author of a commentary on Nahum found in Cave 4 at Qumran refers with horror to the Jewish king Alexander Jannaeus's crucifixion of his opponents, observing that such a thing was 'never done formerly in Israel' (cf. G. Vermes, *The Dead Sea Scrolls in English* [Pelican Books, 1962], p. 232).

[6] Josephus, *War* ii. 261; cf. *Antiquities* xx. 169 ff.

feeding of the multitude in the wilderness east of the Lake of Galilee, the people were minded to take Jesus by force and make him their king. The meeting of the Jewish leaders with the high priest is probably based on John's account of such a meeting after the raising of Lazarus (John 11. 47–53), at which it was decided that Jesus must be put to death. As for the reference to Pilate's wife, who plays a minor part in one of the New Testament trial narratives (Matthew 27. 19), she figures increasingly in Christian fiction.[7]

On the credit side we may place the statement that some people greeted Jesus as the second Moses: that this was so is attested in the New Testament, especially in the Gospel of John.[8]

Another account is given in a further interpolation in the Old Russian translation, in the fifth book of the *Jewish War*, where Josephus gives a description of the Jerusalem temple as it was on the eve of its investment by the Romans. He mentions the notices which warned Gentiles from penetrating beyond the outer court into the inner parts of the temple, and at this point the Old Russian text adds:

Above these inscriptions a fourth inscription was hung in the same letters, which said: 'Jesus, a king who did not reign, was crucified by the Jews because he foretold the destruction of the city and the desolation of the temple.'[9]

As before, the statement that Jesus 'was crucified by the Jews' betrays a non-Jewish origin. The words, 'Jesus, a king who did not reign', form (in Greek) the title of a massive German work by the late Robert Eisler, which appeared in an abridged English edition in 1931 under the title *The Messiah Jesus and John the Baptist*.[10] He regarded the interpolations in the Old Russian version as genuine parts of Josephus's work which were

[7] The one New Testament reference to her (Matthew 27. 19) is considerably expanded in later literature (cf. p. 95); in due course legend provided her with a name—Claudia Procula.

[8] Cf. John 6. 14; 7. 40.

[9] Inserted in *War* v. 195. On the warning notices see p. 202.

[10] R. Eisler, *Iēsous Basileus Ou Basileusas*, 2 volumes (Heidelberg, 1928–9); abridged English translation, *The Messiah Jesus and John the Baptist* (London, 1931).

distorted by Christian copyists and therefore required to be emended so as to be restored to their original form.

By purely subjective emendation Eisler makes several of the statements in the first interpolation quoted above say the opposite of what they appear to say, and argues that Jesus led an unsuccessful revolt against Rome, in the course of which his followers were dispersed and he himself captured and crucified. Eisler's reconstruction, in fact, represents Jesus as doing the very thing which, according to the Gospel narrative, he steadfastly refused to do.

Eisler's argument is presented with such extraordinary erudition and fascinating brilliance that the unwary reader might easily be misled by it; it is important to emphasise that it rests upon his own arbitrary recasting of texts which say the opposite of what he makes them say and which in any case are devoid of any ascertainable historical authority. Unfortunately in some popular re-tellings of the story of Jesus his reconstruction has been presented as though it marked an epoch-making break-through in historical and literary criticism — which it does not.

References to John the Baptist

Two further interpolations in the Old Russian version claim to give fuller details about John the Baptist than the brief account quoted above from the genuine writings of Josephus.

In the second book of the *War*, where Josephus records how Archelaus became ruler of Judaea in 4 B.C. in succession to his father Herod the Great (cf. Matthew 2. 22), we find this interpolation:

At that time there was a man who went about in Judaea clothed in astonishing garments, for he wore animals' hair on his body where he was not covered with his own hair, and his appearance was unkempt. He came among the Jews and summoned them to freedom, saying: 'God has sent me to show you the Way of the Law, by which you will be delivered from having many masters. No longer will you have any mortal master over you, but only the Most High, who has sent me.' When he people heard these words, they were glad, and all Judaea flocked to him, and the region around

Jerusalem. But all that he did to them was to dip them in the stream of the Jordan; then he sent them home, telling them to cease doing evil, and they would be given a king who would liberate them and subdue all who would not submit to him, but he himself would be subject to none. Some mocked at his words, but others believed in him. He was brought before Archelaus, and the doctors of the law gathered together. He was asked who he was and where he had been up to then. He answered: 'I am the man that the Spirit of God has appointed me to be; I feed on rushes and roots and carob-pods.' They threatened to put him to the torture if he did not give up these words and deeds, and he said: 'It is you who ought to give up your unclean deeds and cleave to the Lord your God.' Then a scribe named Simon, an Essene by origin,[11] rose up in anger and said: 'We read the inspired scriptures every day; and do you, who have just come forth to-day like a wild beast from the forest, presume to teach us and lead the people astray with your impious words?' And he rushed upon him to rend his body. But the man rebuked them and said: 'I will not divulge to you the secret which is among you, since you have desired it not. Thus by your own fault an indescribable disaster has come upon you.' So saying he went off to the other side of Jordan, and continued to do as he had done before, without any attempt at hindering him.[12]

This curious narrative does not give a name to the strange man whom it describes. It includes some reminiscences of the biblical account of John the Baptist, but these have been transmitted in a form which made John a vegetarian and turned the locusts on which he fed (Mark 1. 6) into locust-beans or carob-pods (the 'husks' which the prodigal in the parable was reduced to eating).[13] Moreover, they are evidently confused and mixed up with traditions of one or more insurgent leaders such as appeared in great numbers at the time of Herod the Great's death (4 B.C.). The confusion may be seen from the

[11] He may be intended to be identified with Simon the Essene who interpreted a dream of Archelaus and foretold his banishment (Josephus, *War* ii. 113; *Antiquities* xvii. 346 f.).
[12] Immediately after *War* ii. 110.
[13] Luke 15. 16. For John's alleged vegetarianism cf. p. 106 f.

fact that John the Baptist, according to Josephus and the New Testament, was active in the later years of the rule of Antipas (4 B.C.–A.D. 39), not during the reign of Archelaus (4 B.C.–A.D. 6); indeed, according to the first chapter of Luke's Gospel, John was only six months older than Jesus, and would therefore have been a small child at the time of Herod the Great's death.

Dr. Eisler, however, argued that the New Testament was mistaken in its time-indication of the birth and activity of John, and that this interpolation of doubtful origin had preserved a more accurate account. He also identified John, as described in this interpolation, with the Teacher of Righteousness of the Dead Sea Scrolls, the first organiser of the Qumran sect.[14] These fantasies need not detain us. The interpolation itself is probably not a pure invention; it rather represents a confused amalgamation of various traditions of religious and political leaders who arose in Judaea around that time. But its positive historical value is practically nil.

Later in the second book of the *War*, where Josephus mentions that part of Herod the Great's kingdom passed to his son Philip the tetrarch, this interpolation occurs:

> During his administration, Philip had a dream, in which an eagle plucked out both his eyes. He called all his wise men together. When they had all given different interpretations of the dream, there appeared before him suddenly, without being summoned, that man whom we have described above as being dressed in animals' hair and cleansing the people in the waters of Jordan. He said: 'Hear the word of the Lord. As for this dream which you have had, the eagle is your love of money, for this is a violent bird of prey; and the eyes which this sin will take away from you are your dominion and your wife.' So he spoke. Before it was evening, Philip departed this life, and his dominion passed to Agrippa, while his wife Herodias was taken by his brother Herod. Because

---

[14] It must be said in fairness that Eisler based this identification on the only document known to him which mentioned the Teacher of Righteousness: the 'Zadokite Work' found in the synagogue *genizah* (store-room) of Old Cairo early in the twentieth century and first published in 1910. The texts found at Qumran, north-west of the Dead Sea, in 1947 and the following years, make it plain that the Teacher of Righteousness antedated John by at least a century. See p. 67 ff.

of her, all the doctors of the law abhorred him, but they did not dare to accuse him to his face. Only that man whom they called a wild man appeared before him in wrath and said: 'Because you have married your brother's wife, in contempt of the law, the sickle of heaven will cut you down just as your brother died without mercy. The decree of God will not pass over this in silence, but will bring you to your death through sore afflictions in foreign parts, because you are not raising up seed to your brother but satisfying a carnal and adulterous desire, since your brother left four children.'[15] On hearing these words, Herod fell into hot anger and commanded the man to be beaten and chased away. But he would not desist; wherever he came upon Herod, he continued with his accusations, until Herod lost his patience and had him beheaded. Now that man's nature was strange and his ways were not those of ordinary men. He lived like a bodiless spirit.[16] No bread passed his lips; even at the passover he did not taste the unleavened bread, saying: 'It is in remembrance of God, who saved the people from captivity, that they were given this bread to eat, and because the way to freedom was short.' As for wine and strong drink, he would not even let them come near him, and all animal flesh he abhorred.[17] He confounded all unrighteous behaviour; and he lived on carob-pods.[18]

This is a legendary expansion of the Gospel narrative of John the Baptist's relations with Herod Antipas, tetrarch of Galilee and Peraea (cf. Mark 6. 17-29). It includes some historical reminiscences which are not found in the New Testament — e.g. that Philip the tetrarch was succeeded in his principality by the elder Agrippa. Philip died in A.D. 34, and three years later his tetrarchy was bestowed on his nephew Agrippa by the Roman Emperor. But there are grave historical errors in the passage; the interpolator thinks that Herodias's

[15] The part played here by the 'wild man' resembles in some degree Simon the Essene's interpretation of Archelaus's dream (see p. 47, n. 11). As Archelaus was exiled in A.D. 6, so was Herod Antipas in A.D. 39.

[16] For the expression 'bodiless spirit', cf. p. 104.

[17] Cf. Luke 1. 15, also the words of Jesus in Luke 7. 33: 'John the Baptist has come eating no bread and drinking no wine.' See also pp. 47, 106 f., for John's alleged avoidance of animal flesh.

[18] Immediately after *War* ii. 168.

first husband was Philip the tetrarch, whereas he was another son of Herod the Great, Herod Philip by name,[19] who occupied no official position but lived as a private citizen. And it was not after her first husband's death that she married his brother Antipas (which even so would have been illegal, except under the provisions of levirate marriage),[20] but during his lifetime. It was Salome, daughter of Herodias by her first marriage, who became the wife of Philip the tetrarch. Plainly a passage marred by this kind of inaccuracy cannot be taken seriously as a historical source; and if one thing is more obvious than another, it is that Josephus (who was exceptionally well informed about the Herod family and has given us a true and detailed account of these events) had nothing to do with this garbled version.

Other Interpolations

Among the remaining interpolations in the Old Russian version there are three which have some bearing on early Christianity. The first of these, inserted in the second book of the *Jewish War*, follows the account of the death of Herod Agrippa I at Caesarea in A.D. 44 (cf. Acts 12. 23) and his replacement by the procurators Cuspius Fadus and (after him) Tiberius Julius Alexander.

In the time of those rulers many followers of the miracle-worker appeared and spoke to the people about their Master. 'He is alive,' they said, 'although he was dead; and he will set you free from your bondage.' Many of the multitude listened to their preaching and paid heed to their advice — not because of their reputation, for they were of rather humble rank, some tailors, others sandal-makers, others artisans. But the signs which they wrought were wonderful, whatsoever they wished.

But when these noble procurators saw the people falling away, they, in concert with the scribes, determined to seize them and put them to death, for fear that the little might not

[19] 'Herod' according to Josephus (*War* i. 557, 562, etc.; *Antiquities* xvii. 14, 19, etc.), 'Philip' according to Mark (6. 17), followed by Matthew (14. 3).
[20] The levirate marriage (i.e. marriage of a widow to her late husband's brother) was permitted in the law of Israel only when there was no child by the first marriage (Deuteronomy 25. 5–10); otherwise it was forbidden (Leviticus 18. 16; 20. 21). Cf. Mark 12. 18 ff.

remain little, but might end in much. But they shrank back and were in terror at the signs. 'It is not through sorcery (?)', they said, 'that such wonders come to pass; but if they do not proceed from the counsel of God, then they will quickly be exposed.' And they gave them liberty to go where they wished. But later, because of the deeds which they did, they sent them away—some to Caesar, some to Antioch to be tried, others to distant lands.[21]

The interpolator misunderstands Josephus as implying that Fadus and Alexander were joint-procurators; Josephus makes it plain that the latter succeeded the former. For the rest, this account of Christian activity in Judaea during the principate of Claudius is uncorroborated,[22] and in view of the general character of these interpolations it would be unwise to take it very seriously. The remark that if the wonders performed by the Christians 'do not proceed from the counsel of God, then they will quickly be exposed' may well be drawn from Gamaliel's advice to the Sanhedrin regarding the apostles' preaching: 'if this plan or this undertaking is of man, it will fail; but if it is of God, you will not be able to overthrow them' (Acts 5. 38 f.). The only Jewish Christian known to us who was sent to Caesar by a procurator of Judaea was Paul, and he was sent by Festus to Nero (c. A.D. 59) when he exercised his right as a Roman citizen to have his case heard by the emperor (Acts 25. 11 f.).

The second passage, inserted in the fifth book, where Josephus describes the magnificent curtain which hung at the entrance to the temple, adds this note:

This curtain was in perfect condition before the present generation, because the people were pious; but now it presented a sad sight, for it was suddenly torn asunder from top to bottom, when they through bribery handed over to death the benefactor of men, one who (to judge by his actions) was no mere man.[23]

---

[21] Replacing *War* ii. 221 f.
[22] See, however, pp. 196 ff.
[23] After *War* v. 514.

This is simply a Christian importation into Josephus's detailed description of the temple of the statement in the Synoptic Gospels that, at the moment of Jesus's death, 'the curtain of the temple was torn in two, from top to bottom' (Mark 15. 38 and parallels). The description of Jesus is based on the first interpolation quoted in this chapter.

In the Old Russian version this passage is followed by what appears to be an insertion of a later interpolator:

> And they tell of many other dread signs which happened at that time. Then, it was said, after being killed and put in the grave he was not found. Some hold that he had risen, others that he was stolen away by his friends. But for my part I do not know which of these speak more correctly. For one who is dead cannot rise of his own accord (though he may do so when helped by the prayer of another righteous man), unless he is an angel or another of the heavenly powers, or unless God himself appears as a man and accomplishes what he will, and walks with men and falls and lies down and rises again, as he so pleases. But others said that it was not possible to steal him away, because they had set guards round his tomb, thirty Romans and a thousand Jews.[24]

This insertion is dependent on Matthew's passion and resurrection narrative, from which it draws the 'other dread signs' which coincided with Jesus's death (the shaking earth, the rending rocks, the opening tombs and the appearing of 'many bodies of the saints', Matthew 27. 51b–53), the guards at Jesus's tomb (27. 65 ff.) and the report that his body had been stolen (28. 11–15). The professed ignorance of which account is the more correct is not the interpolator's own sentiment, but one which he judged appropriate for Josephus. His own sentiment is plain enough: the body could not have been stolen, because the tomb was so securely guarded; Jesus truly rose, for in him God appeared on earth as a man.

After this insertion the previous passage about the tearing of the curtain is rounded off (presumably by the first interpolator) with the words:

---

[24] This passage is absent from the seventeenth-century Romanian version (based on a Polish translation of the Old Russian).

Such things they declare concerning that curtain . . .

The third passage comes in the course of the sixth book, where Josephus mentions the expected emergence of a world-ruler from Judaea, and says that in his opinion the expectation was fulfilled in Vespasian.[25] The interpolation in the Old Russian version adds:

Some understood this to mean Herod, others the crucified miracle-worker Jesus, others again Vespasian.[26]

Even if we cannot ascribe this addition to Josephus himself, it may well represent the true state of affairs. Josephus may have been the only Jew who applied the oracle about the world-ruler to Vespasian, but Romans who heard about the oracle took it for granted that Vespasian was meant. If, as is probable, 'Herod' is Herod the Great (37–4 B.C.), this could be linked with Herod's fierce reaction to the report of the 'wise men' that the King of the Jews had just been born (Matthew 2. 3 ff.). Herod perhaps cherished imperial or 'messianic' ambitions himself at one time.[27]

If the oracle is Genesis 49. 10, then, although it is not expressly applied to 'the crucified miracle-worker Jesus' in the New Testament, it was interpreted of the Messiah of David's line in the Qumran literature, and became a well-established Christian proof-text from the early second century A.D.

---

[25] See p. 32.
[26] Replacing *War* vi. 313.
[27] An earlier Old Russian interpolation (replacing *War* i. 364–70) depicts some Jewish priests debating whether or not Herod might be the Messiah, and concluding that he was not.

Chapter Four

Jesus in Rabbinical Tradition

THERE are other references to Jesus in Jewish literature beyond those found in the writings of Josephus. He is mentioned, expressly or allusively, in a number of places in the earlier rabbinical literature.

After the fall of the temple and city of Jerusalem in A.D. 70, which brought to an end the second Jewish Commonwealth and its chief-priestly aristocracy, a complete work of reconstruction was necessary if the national unity was to survive. This reconstruction was carried out by men who had belonged to one of the leading Pharisaic schools of the period preceding the disaster—the school of Hillel.[1] By Roman permission these men established their headquarters at Yabneh or Jamnia in western Palestine, under the leadership of Yohanan ben Zakkai.

Here they reconstituted the Sanhedrin as a supreme court for the organisation of the whole range of religious law, with Yohanan as its first president in its new form. A great body of case-law, 'the tradition of the elders' mentioned in the New Testament, had been handed down orally from generation to generation, increasing with the years. The first step towards codifying all this material was now taken. The second step was taken by the great Rabbi Akiba, who was the first to arrange it according to subject-matter. After his death in A.D. 135, on the defeat of Ben-Kosebah's rebellion against Rome,[2] his work was revised and continued by his pupil Rabbi Meir. The work of codification was brought to completion about A.D. 200 by Rabbi

[1] Hillel, founder of the school, flourished in the reign of Herod the Great, about 10 B.C. His successor as head of the school was Gamaliel, the teacher of Saul of Tarsus, 'who is also called Paul' (cf. Acts 5. 34; 22. 3).

[2] Simeon Ben-Kosebah, who led the second Jewish revolt against Rome in A.D. 132, was known to his followers as Bar-Kokhba, 'son of the star', after Akiba had acclaimed him as the 'star out of Jacob' in Balaam's oracle of Numbers 24. 17—i.e. the Messiah.

Judah, president of the Sanhedrin from 170 to 217. The whole of the religious jurisprudence thus compiled is known as the Mishnah.[3]

A parallel compilation of tradition from the same general period is that which bears the title *Tosefta*, meaning 'addition' or 'supplement'.

The completed Mishnah itself became an object of study, and a body of commentary grew up around it in the rabbinical schools both of Palestine and of Babylonia. These commentaries, or Gemaras, formed a sort of supplement to the Mishnah, and Mishnah and Gemara together are usually known as the Talmud. The Jerusalem or Palestinian Talmud, consisting of the Mishnah together with the accumulated Gemara of the Palestinian schools, was completed about A.D. 350; the much larger Babylonian Talmud continued to grow for some generations more, before it was reduced to writing about the year 500.

Another way in which this traditional material was organised was in the form of Midrashim or rabbinical commentaries on books of the Bible.[4]

The period between A.D. 70 and 200 is known as the Tannaitic period, because the rabbis of those years are called the *Tanna'im*, the 'repeaters' of the traditions codified in the Mishnah or Tosefta towards the end of the period. From the Tannaitic period come also the traditions called *baraithoth* (plural of *baraitha*), material 'external' to the Mishnah but preserved in the Gemara.

It is from the Tannaitic period that we should expect the most reliable traditions about Jesus, if indeed any traditions about him are to be found in the rabbinical literature at all. We do in fact find one or two traditions about him, but not much. The most important is a *baraitha* preserved in the Talmudic tractate *Sanhedrin* (43a):

[3] The Mishnah comprises 63 tractates, grouped in six 'Orders', providing in turn a skeleton for the Talmud, which is organised on the same basis. Unless otherwise specified, Talmudic quotations in the following pages are from tractates in the *Babylonian* Talmud (abbreviation TB).

[4] There are two main bodies of midrash — (*a*) the Tannaitic *midrashim*, Mekhilta (on Exodus), Sifra (on Leviticus) and Sifre (on Numbers and Deuteronomy), and (*b*) *midrashim* of the post-Tannaitic period, on the Pentateuch (Genesis, Exodus, Leviticus, Numbers, Deuteronomy) and the five *Megilloth* or 'Scrolls' (Song of Songs, Ruth, Lamentations, Ecclesiastes, Esther), collectively known as Midrash Rabbah.

Jesus was hanged on Passover Eve. Forty days previously the herald had cried, 'He is being led out for stoning, because he has practised sorcery and led Israel astray and enticed them into apostasy. Whosoever has anything to say in his defence, let him come and declare it.' As nothing was brought forward in his defence, he was hanged on Passover Eve.[5]

To this *baraitha* are appended some remarks by 'Ulla, a later rabbi, who flourished about the end of the third century:

'Ulla said: 'Would you believe that any defence would have been so zealously sought for him? He was a deceiver, and the All-merciful says: "You shall not spare him, neither shall you conceal him."[6] It was different with Jesus, for he was near to the kingship.'

The *baraitha* agrees with the Gospel of John in saying that Jesus was hanged on Passover Eve. The description of Jesus's offence may depend on a tradition going back to Jesus's theological controversies with the scribes of which we read in the Gospels; the charge of 'sorcery', for example, is reminiscent of their argument that he expelled demons by the aid of Beelzebul (Mark 3. 22).[7] The wording of the *baraitha*, however, may reflect the sharpened controversies between the followers of Jesus and the successors of the scribes in the decades following A.D. 70.

What is particularly important is that Jesus is said to have been executed for offences against Jewish religious law, not against Roman law. In fact, nothing is said about the Romans

[5] The Talmud introduces this as an illustrative comment on the prescription in the Mishnah that, when a convicted blasphemer is being led away to execution, 'a herald goes out before him, calling: "So-and-so, the son of So-and-so, is going forth to be stoned for such-and-such an offence. So-and-so and So-and-so are witnesses against him. If anyone knows anything in favour of his acquittal, let him come and plead it"' (*Sanhedrin* 6. 1). A reminiscence of the Romans' reserving of capital jurisdiction to themselves is preserved in a *baraitha* which states that 'forty years before the destruction of the temple the right to inflict the death penalty was taken away from Israel' (TJ *Sanhedrin* 1. 1).

[6] Deuteronomy 13. 9.

[7] Sorcery, indeed, was punishable in Roman law, but Roman and Jewish ideas of what constituted sorcery differed.

here. Had death by crucifixion been explicitly mentioned, then Roman executioners would have been implied, since crucifixion was not a Jewish method of execution, whereas hanging (which could, of course, in a non-Jewish context include crucifixion) is a more general term, and hanging in certain forms was traditionally permitted by Jewish law.[8] The absence of any mention of the Romans is due to the fact that the rabbis whose debates are here recorded were concerned to explicate *Jewish* law, for which purpose the Romans would be irrelevant. Lest it should be thought, however, that the Jewish authorities were eager to have Jesus put to death, the rôle of the herald is emphasised. Far from their leaving no stone unturned to procure Jesus's condemnation and execution, it is implied, every endeavour was made to find evidence in his defence. (Here an apologetic note against the Christians may be detected.) But why, it might be asked, were they so solicitous to find ground for acquitting one who was guilty of sorcery and of inciting others to apostasy? Because, said Rabbi 'Ulla, Jesus was a special case; he was 'near to the kingship'—which probably means that he was related to royalty, with reference to his descent from David.[9]

Jesus is occasionally referred to in the rabbinical literature as Jesus Ben Pantera or Ben Pandira, which looks as if it might mean 'the son of the panther'. The analogy of today's Black Panthers might suggest this as a suitable designation for a militant Zealot, but there is no hint in rabbinical tradition that Jesus was that kind of person. According to Origen,[10] Panther was a surname of Jesus's grandfather Jacob (this was his reply to a Jewish calumny, quoted by Celsus, that Pantheras was the name of a pagan soldier).[11] The most probable account of the matter is that Pantheras, with its variant forms, is a corruption

[8] In Jewish law hanging was not so much a method of execution in itself as a form of treatment reserved in certain cases for the corpses of people who had already been executed otherwise, especially by stoning. Hence in the *baraitha* stoning is mentioned as well as hanging.

[9] Another, less probable, interpretation would be that he had connections with the provincial administration—a possible, though mistaken, inference from the Gospel record of Pilate's reluctance to convict him. Least probable of all is the idea that he had Herodian blood in his veins, as Robert Graves suggested in *King Jesus* (London, 1946), pp. 47 ff.

[10] As quoted by Epiphanius, *Heresies*, 78.

[11] Origen, *Against Celsus* i. 32 f. See p. 175, n. 19.

of *parthenos*, the Greek word for 'virgin', and arose from Christian references to Jesus as 'the son of the virgin'.[12]

Sometimes it has been thought that the Talmud also refers to Jesus under the name Ben Stada, who likewise was put to death for sorcery and incitement to apostasy—but at Lydda.[13] There is no ground for identifying Ben Stada and Jesus. Since Ben Stada is said to have imported his apparatus of sorcery from Egypt, it is suggested by some that he may have been the Egyptian rabble-rouser of Acts 21. 38, described by Josephus as a charlatan;[14] this is possible but quite uncertain.

There are possible Talmudic references to Mary (Miriam) the mother of Jesus; but these come in the later strata and are confused. One passage which may refer to her speaks of her as a descendant of princes who nevertheless consorted with carpenters;[15] others confuse her with Mary Magdalene, and treat Magdala, the name of the latter Mary's home town, as though it were *megaddela*, an Aramaic word meaning 'hairdresser'.[16]

The name of Balaam, the false prophet of Mesopotamia (Numbers 22–24), may sometimes be used in later strata of the Talmud as a disguise for the name of Jesus; indeed, it is the mother of 'Balaam' who is said, in the passage mentioned above, to have consorted with carpenters. But there is no reason to suppose that all Talmudic references to Balaam are covert allusions to Jesus, and no reason to suppose that any references to him in the Tannaitic or early post-Tannaitic period are to be understood thus. Here is an early post-Tannaitic passage that is frequently quoted (TB *Sanhedrin* 106b):

A certain heretic said to Rabbi Hanina: 'Have you ever heard how old Balaam was?' He replied: 'There is nothing written about it. But from the scripture which says, "Men

[12] Cf. J. Klausner, *Jesus of Nazareth* (London, 1929), pp. 23 f.; he quotes to this effect K. I. Nitzsch and F. Bleek in *Theologische Studien und Kritiken* 13 (1840), p. 116. Klausner gives a reliable and discriminating account of the rabbinical material relating to Jesus in chapter 1 of *Jesus of Nazareth* (pp. 18–54); a fuller but less critical account is given in R. T. Herford, *Christianity in Talmud and Midrash* (London, 1903).
[13] TB *Sanhedrin* 67a; *Shabbath* 104b. In later strata of the Talmud Ben Stada and Ben Pantera are identified, but the earlier rabbis knew better.
[14] Josephus, *War* ii. 261; *Antiquities* xx. 169 ff. See p. 44.
[15] TB *Sanhedrin* 106a.
[16] TB *Hagigah* 4b.

of blood and treachery shall not live out half their days",[17] he must have been thirty-three or thirty-four years old.' 'A good answer!' said the heretic. 'I have seen the chronicle of Balaam, and this is written in it: "Balaam the lame was thirty-three years when Phinehas the brigand killed him".'

Rabbi Hanina, who died in A.D. 232, was a pupil of Rabbi Judah, the final compiler of the Mishnah.[18] The alleged lameness of Balaam (not attested in the biblical record) is mentioned elsewhere in the Talmud.[19] But the equation of Balaam with Jesus here has been urged on the grounds that (a) Jesus was about thirty-three years old at the time of his death and (b) Phinehas the brigand is a palpable parody on the name of Pontius Pilate. But Pontius Pilate does not come into this picture. The word for 'brigand' here is a synonym for Zealot,[20] and Phinehas, grandson of Aaron the priest, was revered as the archetypal Zealot, who took drastic action to check the apostasy when the Israelites, during their wilderness wanderings, joined in the Moabite cult of Baal-peor (Numbers 25. 1–13; Psalm 106. 28–31) — incited thereto by Balaam (Numbers 31. 16). And in the action in which Balaam was killed Phinehas played a leading part (Numbers 31. 6–8). We have, then, a straightforward reference to the death of Balaam; that his alleged age at the time corresponds with the approximate age of Jesus at his death is a coincidence and nothing more. It is out of the question that a venerated hero like Phinehas should be used as cover for such a villain as Pontius Pilate was in Jewish memory.[21]

In the last quoted Talmudic passage Rabbi Hanina's interlocutor was a 'heretic' — the word in the original is *mîn*. There are numerous references to these *minim* in the rabbinic literature, and sometimes the *minim* in question appear to be Jewish Christians. When this is so, we are dealing with the controversies between Jewish Christians and the representatives of what

[17] Psalm 55. 23.
[18] See pp. 54 f.
[19] Cf. TB *Sanhedrin* 105a, where Rabbi Yohanan deduces Balaam's lameness from a fanciful interpretation of Numbers 23. 3.
[20] Aramaic *lista'a*, a loan word from Greek *lēstēs*, frequently used by Josephus of members of the Zealot party.
[21] See p. 23, n. 9.

was now main-stream Judaism in the period after A.D. 70, when Jewish Christians were excluded from the synagogue.[22] Discussions sometimes arise about the status of 'the books of the *minim*', which seem to have included Jewish-Christian Gospels. Derogatory puns on *euangelion*, the Greek word for 'Gospel', are ascribed to rabbis of the Tannaitic period: they called it '*awen-gillayon* or '*awon-gillayon*, which means something like 'falsehood of the scroll' or 'perversion of the scroll'.[23] Any claim that such works should be granted canonical recognition was decisively rejected. Some rabbis thought they might well be burnt; others suggested that the occurrences of the name of God which they contained should be cut out first.[24]

One reference to an *euangelion* is interesting because it includes a saying similar to one in Jesus's Sermon on the Mount. Rabbi Gamaliel II and his sister Imma Shalom are said to have set a trap for a judge who was notorious for his refusal to take bribes. The judge is called a 'philosopher', which probably implies heretical tendencies. The question on which they tested him was whether a daughter should share the family inheritance equally with a son. (The death of their father Simeon, son of the great Gamaliel, shortly after A.D. 70 could have provided a setting for the story.) The Old Testament law makes it clear enough that daughters could inherit, under certain limiting conditions, only where there were no sons.[25] On this occasion both sister and brother, one after the other, tempted the judge with a bribe (TB *Shabbath* 116a–b):

Imma Shalom sent him a golden lamp. When they came before him, she said: 'Please divide to me the property of the women's quarters.' He said to them: 'Divide it so.' They said to him: 'For us it is written: "Where there is a son, a daughter does not inherit."' He said to them: 'Since the day that you were exiled from your land[26] the law of Moses has been abrogated, and the law of the *euangelion* has been given, in

[22] Cf. F. F. Bruce, *The Spreading Flame* (Paternoster Press, 1958), p. 267; *New Testament History* (Oliphants, 1969), pp. 365 f.

[23] Cf. TB *Shabbath* 116a.

[24] Cf. Tosefta, *Shabbath* 13. 5; TB *Shabbath* 116a.

[25] The limiting conditions restricted their freedom in marriage to men of their own tribe (Numbers 36. 1–12).

[26] Presumably since the disaster of A.D. 70.

which it is written: "A son and daughter shall inherit alike."'
Next day Gamaliel sent him a Libyan ass. The judge then
said to them: 'I have looked further to the end of the book,
and in it is written: "I have not come to take away from the
law of Moses, and I have not come to add to the law of
Moses." Now in the law of Moses it is written: "Where
there is a son, a daughter does not inherit."' She said to him:
'Let your light shine as a lamp.' Rabban Gamaliel said to her:
'The ass has come and trodden out the lamp.'[27]

It is implied, though not stated in so many words, in the Old
Testament law, that a daughter inherits only where there is no
son. This is made clear by Moses's ruling in the case of the
daughters of Zelophehad: 'If a man dies, and has no son, then
you shall cause his inheritance to pass to his daughter' (Numbers
27. 8). But in this story the judge first quoted, in favour of
Imma Shalom, a new ruling which superseded that of Moses,
though what the *euangelion* was in which he found it we cannot
say. Later, however, he was moved to give a ruling more in
favour of Gamaliel when he read on in the *euangelion* and found
words which confirmed that the law of Moses must be modified
neither by subtraction nor by addition. These words, 'I have not
come to take away from the law of Moses, and I have not come
to add to the law of Moses',[28] are recognisable as a variation on
Jesus's words in Matthew 5. 17: 'Think not that I have come to
abolish the law and the prophets; I have come not to abolish
them but to fulfil them.'
Imma Shalom, it is interesting to note, was the wife of Rabbi
Eliezer ben Hyrcanus, who was himself later charged with
heresy (*minuth*). Rabbi Eliezer appears to have had some
dealings with Jewish Christians: there is an odd *baraitha* telling
of his meeting one by the name of Jacob from Kefar Sekanya,
who discussed with him the law of Deuteronomy 23. 18: 'You
shall not bring the hire of a harlot . . . into the house of the
Lord your God in payment for any vow.' Jacob expressed the
judgment, apparently on the authority of Jesus, that if money

[27] The second bribe was more persuasive than the first. (Rabban is a more
honorific term, given to specially outstanding rabbis.)
[28] Some would read this 'I have not come to take away but (Aramic *'ella*
instead of *we-la*, "and not") to add'; but the text as given above is required
by the context.

paid into the sacred treasury was later discovered to come from such a tainted source, it could be used to construct a latrine for the high priest.[29]

It may be the same Jacob who appears in another *baraitha* as coming to heal a fellow-rabbi, also called Eliezer (ben Dama), of snakebite in the name of Jesus ben Pantera. Eliezer's uncle, Rabbi Ishmael, forbade him to submit to the cure, and Eliezer undertook to prove from the law that he was permitted to do so, but died before he could quote the verse. Rabbi Ishmael congratulated the dead man that he had departed in peace, as he would not have done had he accepted restoration to health in the name of Jesus.[30]

The most noteworthy Talmudic account of Jesus's disciples comes in a *baraitha* which follows immediately on the account of Jesus's execution in TB *Sanhedrin* 43a.[31]

The rabbis taught:

Jesus had five disciples: Mathai, Naqai, Nezer, Buni and Todah.

When Mathai was brought before the court, he said to them, 'Should Mathai be put to death, since it is written: "I, Mathai, shall come and appear before God"?'[32] They answered him, 'Yes; Mathai shall be put to death, since it is written: "Mathai shall die, and his name perish."'[33]

When Naqai was brought before them, he said to them, 'Should Naqai be put to death, since it is written: "Naqai and the righteous thou shalt not put to death"?'[34] They answered him, 'Yes; Naqai shall be put to death, since it is written: "In secret places he slays Naqai."'[35]

When Nezer was brought before them, he said to them, 'Should Nezer be put to death, since it is written: "Nezer shall grow out of his roots"?'[36] They answered him, 'Yes;

---

[29] TB *Abodah Zarah* 16b–17a.

[30] Tosefta, *Hullin* 2. 22 f.; TB *Abodah Zarah* 27b.

[31] See p. 56.

[32] Psalm 42. 2: 'when (*mathai*) shall I come and appear before God?'

[33] Psalm 41. 5: 'when (*mathai*) will he die and his name perish?'

[34] Exodus 23. 7: 'the innocent (*naqi*) and the righteous thou shalt not put to death'.

[35] Psalm 10. 8: 'in secret places he slays the innocent (*naqi*)'. Perhaps in the rabbinical word-play *naqi* was treated as the subject of the verb: 'in secret places Naqai commits murder'—and therefore deserves to die.

[36] Isaiah 11. 1: 'a branch (*nezer*) shall grow out of his roots'.

Nezer shall be put to death, since it is written: "But you are cast forth [from your tomb] like abominable Nezer."[37]

When Buni was brought before them, he said to them, 'Should Buni be put to death, since it is written: "Buni, my firstborn, is Israel" ?'[38] They answered him, 'Yes; Buni shall be put to death, since it is written: "I will kill your firstborn Buni."'[39]

When Todah was brought before them, he said to them, 'Should Todah be put to death, since it is written: "A psalm for Todah" ?'[40] They answered him, 'Yes; Todah shall be put to death, since it is written: "He who sacrifices Todah honours me."'[41]

Most of this story about the five disciples is a rabbinical game, in which the disciples and their judges engage in competitive word-play by treating a common word in some familiar passage of Hebrew scripture as a personal name. It has no historical value. Of the disciples' names Mathai is easily identified with Matthew and Todah, perhaps, with Thaddaeus (Mark 3. 18 // Matthew 10. 3). Naqai could conceivably represent a shortened form of Nicodemus, and Buni might be a shortened form of Boanerges, the sobriquet given by Jesus to the brothers James and John, explained in Mark 3. 8 as meaning 'sons of thunder' (Aramaic *benê regesh*). Nezer is probably related to 'Nazarene', a title first given to Jesus and then also to his followers (cf. Acts 24. 5). The text which Nezer invokes in his defence, 'A branch (*nezer*) shall grow out of his roots' (Isaiah 11. 1), comes from an oracle foretelling the rise of the ideal prince of the house of David (who came in the intertestamental period to be called the Messiah without further qualification); it may be the text indicated by the enigmatic statement in Matthew 2. 23, that the infant Jesus was taken to reside in Nazareth 'that what was spoken by the prophets might be fulfilled, "He shall be called a Nazarene"' (as though the vowels of *nezer*, 'branch', were replaced by those of *nozri*, 'Nazarene').

[37] Isaiah 14. 19: 'but you are cast out . . . like an abominable branch (*nezer*)'.

[38] Exodus 4. 22: 'My son (*beni*), my firstborn, is Israel.'

[39] Exodus 4. 23: 'I will kill your son (*binekha*), your firstborn.'

[40] Psalm 100, superscription: 'A psalm for the thank-offering (*todah*).'

[41] Psalm 50. 23: 'He who brings thanksgiving (*todah*) as his sacrifice honours me.'

Why only five disciples instead of the conventional twelve? One suggestion is that they are somehow related to the five disciples called by Jesus in the narrative of John 1. 35–51 – Andrew, Simon Peter, Philip, Nathanael and an unnamed disciple. This is quite unlikely: none of the names can be made to correspond.

Jesus acquired another disciple, much later than the others, in Saul of Tarsus, better known as Paul, apostle of the Gentiles. In his younger days he was a pupil of the elder Gamaliel, and gave practical evidence of his zeal for the ancestral law of Israel by his campaign against the infant church.[42] Had he persisted in his original course, his name would have figured prominently in rabbinic tradition. Does it figure at all?

Professor Joseph Klausner thought perhaps it did.[43]

Rabbinical tradition knows of a pupil of Gamaliel – referred to simply as 'that pupil' – who manifested 'impudence in matters of learning'. When Gamaliel expounded Scripture so as to show what wonders would be seen on earth in coming days, 'that pupil' scoffed at him and denied that such wonders could be expected, since 'there is nothing new under the sun' (Ecclesiastes 1. 9). But on each occasion Gamaliel proved that the wonders had their counterpart in the present world.[44] There is nothing here which points specially to Paul, but if a distinguished pupil of Gamaliel's went wrong in later years there would be a tendency in rabbinical folklore to read his later apostasy from the law back into his undergraduate days. Klausner's suggestion is possible: more than that cannot be said.

There was a good deal of contact between orthodox Jews and Jewish Christians in Palestine in the first and second centuries, and there are frequent echoes in the rabbinical literature of controversies between the two parties, on the interpretation of messianic prophecy, for example. In a number of instances interpretations which had formerly been regarded as quite proper and respectable by orthodox Jews were ruled out as inadmissible when Christians began to use them to prove that Jesus was the Messiah.

There is one notable occasion recorded when the great Rabbi

[42] Cf. Galatians 1. 13 f.; Acts 22. 3–5.
[43] *From Jesus to Paul* (London, 1944), pp. 309 ff.
[44] TB *Shabbath* 30b.

Akiba got into trouble because he favoured such an unacceptable interpretation. He and his colleagues were discussing the vision of the judgment day in Daniel 7. 9–14, where 'one like a son of man' appears before the Ancient of Days to receive universal and eternal sovereignty from him. 'As I looked', says Daniel (verse 9), 'thrones were placed, and one that was ancient of days took his seat.' The question was raised: Why thrones in the plural? Akiba gave the traditional answer: 'One for God and one for David' (i.e. for Messiah, the son of David). But Rabbi José expostulated with him: 'Akiba, how long will you profane the Shekhinah? It is one for justice and one for righteousness.'[45]

Ever since Jesus had claimed, at his trial before the Sanhedrin, to be that Son of Man whom Daniel saw 'coming with the clouds of heaven' the messianic interpretation of the passage had become taboo for many Jewish teachers.

The rabbis of this period, then, were not unacquainted with the story of Jesus and the activity of his followers, vigorously as they voiced their dissent from all that he and they stood for.

---

[45] TB *Sanhedrin* 38b; *Hagigah* 14a. Another interpretation, more acceptable than the traditional one, proposed in the same context is that one throne was for the Ancient of Days to sit on and another to serve as his footstool. Akiba may have had in mind the divine invitation to the Messiah in Psalm 110. 1: 'Sit at my right hand, till I make your enemies your footstool' — but the fact that Jesus in his reply to the high priest at his trial had conjoined this text with Daniel 7. 13 meant that its former messianic interpretation also was no longer favoured.

Chapter Five

Preparation for the Messiah

Qumran and the Teacher of Righteousness

THERE is another body of Jewish literature which has attracted much publicity since it was first discovered in 1947. That is the collection of texts popularly called the Dead Sea Scrolls, and more particularly the documents found in eleven caves in the region of Qumran, on the north-west shore of the Dead Sea. The Qumran documents appear to have come from an ascetic community of pious Jews which had its headquarters in that region for some two centuries, until those headquarters were destroyed during the Roman suppression of the Jewish revolt which broke out in A.D. 66.[1] Those headquarters, a complex of buildings known locally as Khirbet Qumran, were thoroughly excavated in the 1950s, and it seems reasonably certain that they should be identified with the Essene centre 'above Engedi' which the elder Pliny mentions shortly after A.D. 70 in his *Natural History*.[2]

The question has repeatedly been raised if the Qumran documents make any reference to Jesus or Christian origins. The answer is No. Nor should that surprise us. The Qumran community withdrew as far as possible from public life and lived in its wilderness retreat; Jesus carried on his ministry in places where people lived and worked, mixing with all sorts and conditions, and by preference (it appears) with men and women whose society pious men like those of Qumran would rather avoid. And, more important still, practically all the

[1] I have dealt more fully with this subject in *Second Thoughts on the Dead Sea Scrolls* (Paternoster Press, 3rd edition, 1966). A useful translation of the main Qumran texts is available in G. Vermes, *The Dead Sea Scrolls in English* (Pelican Books, 1962), referred to in the following footnotes as 'Vermes'.

[2] Pliny, *Natural History* v. 73. (The elder Pliny, who met his death in the eruption of Vesuvius in A.D. 79, was uncle to the younger Pliny, mentioned above on pp. 23 ff.)

Qumran texts dealing with religious topics (so far as they have been published to date) are assigned on palaeographical grounds[3] to the pre-Christian decades. In the latest of them the messianic age is yet to come; the New Testament is dominated by the proclamation that it has come.

Yet the importance of the Qumran documents for the study of Christian beginnings is very great. They have provided a new background against which practically every book of the New Testament can be read in some part at least with fresh understanding.

The community to which these documents belonged appears to have been organised about 150 B.C. or shortly afterwards by a leader who is never explicitly named but is regularly referred to by a Hebrew phrase commonly translated the Teacher of Righteousness. The title may have been derived from Hosea 10. 12 and Joel 2. 23, in each of which passages there is a Hebrew expression, actually denoting beneficial showers of rain, which has at times been taken to signify the teaching of righteousness.[4] It may be, on the other hand, that the designation at Qumran means 'rightful guide' — but in practice it does not matter, for in the eyes of his followers the community's first leader was both a rightful guide and a teacher of righteousness.

At the beginning of the *Zadokite Work*, the one document emanating from the Qumran community which was known before the manuscript discoveries,[5] it is recorded how, in a time of national apostasy,

God . . . remembered the covenant of the forefathers and caused a remnant to remain for Israel and did not give them

[3] Palaeography is ancient handwriting; given a sufficient amount of manuscript material, it is possible to assign dates to it within reasonable limits on the basis of the development of handwriting styles from one generation to another.

[4] In Joel 2. 23 the margin of the Authorized Version actually gives 'a teacher of righteousness' as an alternative rendering.

[5] See p. 48, n. 14. Two imperfect manuscripts of this *Zadokite Work* (so called because it maintains the high-priestly rights of the house of Zadok) were discovered in the store-room of an ancient synagogue in Old Cairo early in the present century: the origin of the work remained obscure until further fragments were identified among the Qumran manuscripts. (It is sometimes called the *Damascus Document*, because of references to Damascus found in the text.)

up to be consumed. And in the epoch of wrath, 390 years[6] after he gave them into the power of Nebuchadnezzar, king of Babylon, he visited them; and he caused to sprout from Israel and from Aaron[7] a root of [his] planting to possess his land and to grow fat in the goodness of his soil. They considered their iniquity and knew that they were guilty men; but they were like blind men, groping for a way, for twenty years. Then God took note of their deeds, for they sought him with a perfect heart, and he raised up for them a teacher of righteousness to lead them in the way of his heart, that he might make known to the last generations what he was about to do to the last generation — the congregation of deceivers.[8]

Later references in the *Zadokite Work* make it plain that salvation is to be found only in following the directions of this Teacher of Righteousness:

All who hold fast to these rules, to go out and come in according to the law, and who listen to the voice of the Teacher, and make confession before God, saying, 'In truth we have acted wickedly, both we and our fathers, by walking contrary to the ordinances of the covenant; just and true are your judgments against us'; who do not wilfully contravene his holy ordinances, righteous judgments and truthful testimonies; who learn from the former judgments which the men of the community endured; who pay heed to the voice of the Teacher of Righteousness, and do not repudiate the righteous ordinances when they hear them — they will rejoice and be glad, and their hearts will be strong, and they will gain dominion over all the children of the world, and God will make propitiation for them, and they will see his salvation, for they have trusted in his holy name.[9]

The evidence of the *Zadokite Work* tallies with much that is said about the Teacher of Righteousness in commentaries on

---

[6] Cf. Ezekiel 4. 5.
[7] That is, from the laity and the priesthood (both together making up the people of God).
[8] CD 1. 4–12; cf. Vermes, p. 97.
[9] CD 20. 27–34; cf. Vermes, pp. 107 f.

various biblical texts found in the Qumran caves. It should be added that the biblical commentaries from Qumran throw no light on the original meaning of the biblical texts, but much light on the beliefs and expectations of the commentators and their associates. Thus there is no discernible relation, except in the commentator's mind, between the words of Micah 1. 5b ('and what are the high places of Judah? are they not Jerusalem?')[10] and the explanation of them in a fragmentary commentary on Micah from Cave 1:

[The interpretation of this con]cerns the Teacher of Righteousness: it is he who [teaches the law to] his [council] and to all those who volunteer to be included among the elect people [of God, practising the law] in the council of the community, who will be saved from the day [of judgment].[11]

To the same effect the commentary on Habakkuk found in Cave 1 expounds as follows the frequently quoted clause 'The righteous shall live by his faith' (Habakkuk 2. 4):

The interpretation of this concerns all the doers of the law in the house of Judah, whom God will save from the place of judgment because of their labour and their faith in the Teacher of Righteousness.[12]

The Teacher of Righteousness was enabled to teach the law of God so unerringly to his followers because of a special illumination from above which made the writings of the prophets luminous to him as they had been to no one previously, not even to the prophets themselves. The warnings of judgment in Habakkuk 1.5 are directed by the Qumran commentator against those who pay no attention to what 'the Teacher of Righteousness [told them] from the mouth of God' and

---

[10] This is the literal rendering of the Hebrew text, which lay before the Qumran commentator. The Revised Standard Version, following other ancient authorities, renders the passage: 'And what is the sin of the house of Judah? Is it not Jerusalem?'

[11] Cf. Vermes, pp. 230 f. The material enclosed within square brackets fills in lacunae in the text.

[12] Cf. Vermes, p. 237.

will not believe when they hear all that is to [come upon] the last generation, from the mouth of the priest into [whose heart] God has put wisdom to interpret all the words of his servants the prophets, [through] whom God told all that was to befall his people and [his land].[13]

It is most natural to identify 'the priest' in this quotation with the Teacher of Righteousness; indeed, in a commentary on the Psalms from Cave 4 he is expressly called 'the priest, the Teacher of Righteousness'.[14]

In Habakkuk 2. 1 f. the prophet tells how, in his concern to understand the divine purpose, he decided to wait for the fresh light which might come as the purpose was further unfolded by the course of events, and how he received the assurance that the final vindication of the rightful cause would not be long delayed. The commentator's exposition of this passage runs as follows:

> God commanded Habakkuk to write the things that were to come upon the last generation, but the fulfilment of the epoch he did not make known to him. As for the words, 'so he may run who reads it', their interpretation concerns the Teacher of Righteousness, to whom God made known all the mysteries of his servants the prophets.[15]

In other words, Habakkuk was enabled by the Spirit of prophecy to foresee what the end-time events would be, but knowledge of the time when they would take place was withheld from him. This 'mystery' was reserved for the Teacher of Righteousness, to whom it was divulged (also by divine revelation)[16] that the time of the end was close at hand and that all the predictions of the Hebrew prophets were about to be fulfilled. There is a New Testament parallel to this in 1 Peter 1. 10 ff. where the prophets who foretold the messianic suffer-

---

[13] Cf. Vermes, p. 233.

[14] On Psalm 37. 24 f.; cf. Vermes, p. 242.

[15] Cf. Vermes, p. 236.

[16] There is a possible reference to this in another Qumran commentary on the Psalms, where the words of Psalm 127. 2, 'he gives (it) to his beloved one in sleep', are somehow related to 'the Teacher of Righteousness, the priest'; but the text is so fragmentary as to make certainty impossible.

ings and subsequent glories are said to have 'searched and enquired' in an attempt to discover what person and what time were indicated by the Spirit of prophecy when he bore witness about these matters in advance. But those, like the writer and his readers, who had believed the gospel had no need to enquire, for they knew: the person was Jesus; the time was now.

The Teacher of Righteousness endured molestation and persecution at the hands of his enemies, one of whom figures with special prominence under the designation of the 'Wicked Priest'. 'Wicked' in this sense means primarily 'illegitimate'; the Teacher and his community believed that the high-priesthood in Jerusalem belonged exclusively to the family of Zadok, which had ministered in the temple (apart from the interruption caused by the Babylonian exile in the sixth century B.C.) from the time of Solomon (c. 950 B.C.) to the deposition of the last Zadokite high priest by Antiochus Epiphanes (c. 168 B.C.). When the high-priesthood was assumed by the Hasmonaean family, the men of Qumran refused to acknowledge its right to do so. The first Hasmonaean to become high priest was Jonathan, brother of Judas Maccabaeus (152 B.C.); the Wicked Priest who persecuted the Teacher is most probably to be identified with Jonathan, or else with one of his successors. But the Teacher survived all his attacks; to him the Psalms commentary from Cave 4 mentioned above applies the words of Psalm 37. 32 f.:

'The wicked watches the righteous, and seeks to slay him. The Lord will not abandon him to his power, or let him be condemned when he is brought to trial.' The interpretation of this concerns the Wicked Priest who watches the righteous one and seeks to slay him . . . and the law which he sent to him. But God will not abandon him and will not condemn him when he is judged; but he will repay the Wicked Priest his recompense by giving him into the power of the terrible Gentiles to execute judgment on him.[17]

These last words may refer to Jonathan, who was kidnapped by his enemies in 143 B.C. and died in captivity. But the Teacher of Righteousness appears to have emerged safely from his

[17] Cf. Vermes, pp. 242 f.

troubles and died in peace. His death is described as his being 'gathered in' — an expression appropriate to a natural death.[18]

Messianic Expectation at Qumran

The Teacher's appearance was regarded as a sign that the last days were at hand. Neither in his own eyes nor in the eyes of his followers was he a messianic figure, but his ministry signified that the messianic age was at hand. We cannot accept his identification with John the Baptist, suggested many years ago by Robert Eisler;[19] still less his identification with Jesus, suggested shortly after the discoveries in the Qumran caves by Dr. J. L. Teicher.[20] But he had this in common with John the Baptist, that both were preparers of the way for the Messiah. Probably it was believed at one time that the messianic age would be the immediate sequel to his ministry, but when he died a revision of this opinion was necessary. An indeterminate interval is indicated in the *Zadokite Work* as elapsing 'from the day when the unique Teacher was gathered in until the rise of a Messiah from Aaron and from Israel'.[21]

The Qumran community was sometimes called the community of 'Aaron and Israel' because it comprised both priests (Aaron) and laymen (Israel). 'A Messiah from Aaron and Israel' should probably be taken to mean a priestly Messiah and a lay Messiah. This is supported by the direction in the *Rule of the Community* (a scroll found in Cave 1) that the members shall abide by their rule 'until the coming of a prophet and the Messiahs of Aaron and Israel'.[22] The reference here is to three

---

[18] Thus in CD 20. 14 f., 'from the day when the unique Teacher was gathered in until the destruction of all the men of war who returned with the man of falsehood is about forty years' (cf. Vermes, p. 107). The 'man of falsehood' was perhaps the leader of a rival religious community, and the destruction of his followers may have been an incident in the reign of the Hasmonaean ruler Alexander Jannaeus (103–76 B.C.).

[19] R. Eisler, *The Messiah Jesus and John the Baptist* (London, 1931), pp. 254 f. See p. 48.

[20] J. L. Teicher, 'The Dead Sea Scrolls—Documents of the Jewish-Christian Sect of Ebionites', *Journal of Jewish Studies* 2 (1951), pp. 67 ff. Dr. Teicher held that the community of the scrolls consisted of Ebionites (see p. 105), whose *bête noire* was Paul, and he proposed that Paul, the erstwhile persecutor of Jewish Christians, was the Wicked Priest. A similar interpretation had been proposed on the basis of the *Zadokite Work* by G. Margoliouth in the *Athenaeum*, No. 4335 (November 26, 1910), p. 657.

[21] CD 19. 35–20. 1; cf. Vermes, p. 106.

[22] 1 QS 9. 11; cf. Vermes, p. 87.

expected figures of the end-time: (i) the prophet like Moses,
foretold in Deuteronomy 18. 15 ff., (ii) the Messiah of David's
line, and (iii) an anointed priest. When the term 'the Messiah'
is used absolutely, it is the coming prince of the house of David
that is meant. He would be a military leader, like his ancestor
David, but in the new age he would be subordinate to the
anointed priest, who would function as head of state. This
arrangement follows that laid down in the blueprint of the new
commonwealth detailed in Ezekiel 40–48, in which 'the prince'
—actually called David (Ezekiel 44. 3; 34. 24)—takes his orders
from the priestly establishment.

One document found in Cave 4 is known as 4Q *Testimonia*
because it brings together 'testimonies' or proof-texts from the
Hebrew Bible relating to these three figures. The first is the
Deuteronomy passage about the prophet like Moses with some
associated passages; the second is Balaam's oracle about the
victorious 'star out of Jacob' and 'sceptre out of Israel' in
Numbers 24. 15–17, which originally referred to King David
and so is appropriately reapplied to 'great David's greater son';
the third is Moses's blessing pronounced on the tribe of Levi
in Deuteronomy 33. 8–11.[23] In that order the three 'testimonies' refer to the prophet, the king and the priest of the
end-time. The priest in this context is not only one who offers
sacrifice but also one who expounds the law, and it is this latter
rôle that is emphasised in the Qumran expectation.

In another document from Cave 4, for example, called 4Q
Florilegium, Nathan's promise to David about the son whom
God will raise up for him (2 Samuel 7. 11–14) is interpreted
thus:

This is the shoot of David who is to arise with the Expounder
of the Law . . . in Zion in the latter days.[24]

As the 'shoot of David' is the Messiah of Israel, so the 'Expounder of the Law' is the Messiah of Aaron.

There is a similar association of these two personages in a

---

[23] Cf. Vermes, pp. 245 f. These three proof-texts are followed by a
fourth, Joshua 6. 26, in which the curse on the rebuilder of Jericho falls on
'an accursed man, a man of Belial' (probably one of the Hasmonaean rulers).

[24] Cf. Vermes, p. 244.

section of the *Zadokite Work* which interprets the oracle of Balaam mentioned above, but does so in such a way as to dissociate the 'star out of Jacob' from the 'sceptre out of Israel' (contrary to 4Q *Testimonia*, in which the two figures are related to one and the same person, in accordance with the meaning of the original text, where they stand in synonymous parallelism). The Zadokite author identifies the 'star' with 'the Expounder of the Law' while the 'sceptre' is said to be 'the prince of all the congregation who, when he comes, will "break down all the sons of tumult"' (cf. Numbers 24. 17).[25]

Like his great ancestor, the 'prince of all the congregation' is a warrior who will crush the enemies of his people. Further details of his crushing them are given in other community documents, and especially in a scroll from Cave 1 called the *Rule of War*, which describes how, in a generation of fighting at the end-time, the 'sons of light' will annihilate all the 'sons of darkness'. Chief among the 'sons of darkness' are the *Kittim*, the last Gentile nation to impose its dominion on Israel. The *Kittim*, who in this context are historically to be equated with the Romans (an equation first found in Daniel 11. 30), are the first of Israel's enemies to be vanquished; this requires a campaign stretching over six years. Once they are crushed, the other enemies can be dealt with more easily. Thus eternal redemption would be achieved, and the kingdom of God established for ever.[26]

When we think of the New Testament Messiah, we tend to associate him not only with the expected prince of the house of David but also—and perhaps even more so—with such figures of Old Testament prophecy as the Servant of the Lord in the book of Isaiah and the Son of Man in the book of Daniel. These figures have not influenced the messianic doctrine of the Qumran community. The designations 'Servant of the Lord' and 'Son of Man' do not appear. But some of the Servant Songs of the book of Isaiah have influenced the thought and wording of several of the Qumran texts and these texts also contain echoes of some of the functions ascribed by Daniel to the 'one

[25] CD 7. 19 f.; cf. Vermes, p. 104. A collection of blessings appended to the *Rule of the Community* includes a blessing for 'the prince of the congregation', who is plainly the coming 'shoot from the stump of Jesse' of Isaiah 11. 1–5 (1QSb 5. 19 ff.); cf. Vermes, pp. 208 f.

[26] Cf. Vermes, pp. 122 ff.

like a son of man' whom he saw in his vision of the day of judgment.[27] We might indeed venture to say that the community, without using either of the designations, envisages itself as filling the rôle of the Servant during its wilderness seclusion and as destined to fill the rôle of the Son of Man when the hour came to march 'to the help of the Lord against the mighty'.

The community consisted of 'volunteers for holiness', and holiness was construed very strictly. No one was compelled to join, but those who did so, after a searching period of probation, had to submit to a severely ascetic discipline. If the Pharisees ('separated people') were so called because they were so careful to avoid people and things that might convey religious pollution, the men of Qumran criticised the Pharisees for not being nearly thorough-going enough in their separation, and dubbed them the 'seekers after smooth things' or 'givers of smooth expositions'—people who preferred lax rather than strict interpretations of the law. We can imagine what they would have thought of Jesus, whom even the Pharisees criticised because, in their eyes, he kept such dubious company and treated the law with such sovereign freedom.

The privations which were involved by the men of Qumran in their painstaking study and practice of the law of God they gladly endured. They endured also the persecution which was visited upon them by the Wicked Priest and their other enemies. For they believed that by enduring all this they would accumulate an excess of righteousness which would be counted to the credit of their erring fellow-Israelites and be accepted by God for the atonement of the land. (Their own righteous status before God, the Teacher taught them, was a gift of divine grace.) This attitude is quite similar to what is said of the Servant of the Lord: 'the righteous one, my servant,. will procure righteousness for the many, and he will bear their iniquities' (Isaiah 53. 11).

But alongside the making of atonement for the land the men of Qumran included in their ministry 'the execution of judgment upon wickedness, so that perversity may be no more'.[28] They could not do this in the period when they were despised

[27] Daniel 7. 13 f.
[28] 1QS 8. 10; cf. Vermes, p. 85.

and rejected. But as the 'one like a son of man' in Daniel's vision is invested with universal sovereignty and the power to execute judgment, so these saints of the Most High looked forward to the day of vindication. In the Habakkuk commentary from Cave 1 the prophet's words, 'Thou hast ordained him to execute judgment; and thou, O Rock, hast established him to inflict chastisement' (Habakkuk 1. 12b), are explained thus:

> The interpretation of this saying is that God will not destroy his people by the hand of the nations, but into the hand of his elect God will commit the judgment of all nations, and by the chastisement which they inflict those who have kept his commandments in the time of their distress will condemn all the wicked of his people.[29]

These, then, were some of the forms of expectation cherished by one pious community in Israel on the eve of the birth of Christianity. Their expectations did not materialise in the way they hoped. When the great conflict with the 'sons of darkness' broke out they were attacked, overrun and dispersed. In dispersion after A.D. 70 they may have made common cause with the exiled church of Jerusalem and contributed some of their distinctive views to the Jewish Christian party of the Ebionites of whom something more will be said in the following chapters.

The Testaments of the Patriarchs

The Testaments of the Twelve Patriarchs is the title given to a group of twelve documents in which each of the twelve sons of Jacob, before his death, gives his descendants exhortations and predictions of their future fortunes. The work as we now have it is a Christian compilation, written in Greek, possibly in the late first or early second century A.D. But some at least of the individual *Testaments* have a Jewish basis: fragments of the *Testament of Levi* (in Aramaic) and the *Testament of Naphtali* (in Hebrew) have been identified among the Qumran texts. The Greek recension, however, is not a straight translation of these Semitic texts.

[29] In the original prophecy it is the Chaldaean oppressor who is so ordained, but the commentary identifies the appointed executor of divine judgment with him 'who is of purer eyes than to behold evil' (Habakkuk 1. 13a); cf. Vermes, p. 235.

In the *Testament of Levi*, as we might expect, the priesthood is magnified, and the rise of the great priest of the end-time is foretold. The priesthood will be eclipsed for a season.

Then the Lord will raise up a new priest
to whom all the words of the Lord will be revealed;
he will execute true judgment on the earth for a
      multitude of days.
His star will rise in heaven like that of a king,
lighting up the light of knowledge like the midday sun . . .
The heavens will be opened
and from the temple of glory sanctification will come
      upon him
with the Father's voice as from Abraham to Isaac.[30]

Alongside the priesthood from the tribe of Levi is the kingship from the tribe of Judah, but as in Qumran expectation the kingship is subordinate to the priesthood. Thus Judah says to his sons:

To me God gave the kingship and to him [Levi] the priesthood, and he set the kingship below the priesthood. To me he gave the things on earth, to him the things in heaven. As heaven is higher than earth, so is God's priesthood greater than earthly kingship . . .[31]

Similarly Naphtali tells his sons how once, in a vision, he saw the sun and moon standing still over the Mount of Olives.

And Isaac, my father's father, said to us: 'Run and take hold of them, each according to his strength, and the sun and moon will belong to him who seizes them.' So we all run together, and Levi took hold of the sun, and Judah outstripped the others and seized the moon; and they were both lifted up with them.[32]

---

[30] *Testament of Levi* 18. 2–6. The mention of Abraham and Isaac may refer to Genesis 22. 7 f., the only place in the Old Testament where Abraham speaks to Isaac.
[31] *Testament of Judah* 21. 2–4.
[32] *Testament of Naphtali* 5. 2 f.

The priesthood is as far superior to the kingship, it is implied, as the sun outshines the moon.

There is a marked deviation from this division of the priesthood and the kingship between Levi and Judah in the *Testament of Reuben*, where Levi is said to be not only 'anointed high priest' but king as well:

He will bless Israel and Judah, because it is he whom the Lord has chosen to be king over all the nation. And bow down before his offspring, for on your behalf they will die in wars visible and invisible. So Levi will be an eternal king among you.[33]

It is a near-certainty that this passage, ascribing kingship as well as priesthood to the tribe of Levi,[34] reflects the situation under the dynasty of the Hasmonaeans, who combined the kingship with the high-priesthood until they lost their secular power with the Roman occupation in 63 B.C.

All this concern with the Levitical priesthood, whether in historical times or, by expectation, at the end-time, has nothing to do with the messianic ministry ascribed to Jesus in the New Testament. According to the one New Testament writer who speaks of Jesus's ministry in terms of high-priesthood, 'it is evident that our Lord was descended from Judah, and in connection with that tribe Moses said nothing about priests' (Hebrews 7. 14). When, therefore, the writer to the Hebrews seeks Old Testament authority for his exposition of Jesus's heavenly priesthood he finds it not in any reference to the tribe of Levi but in an oracle in the Psalter where the anointed king of David's line is divinely acclaimed as 'a priest for ever after the order of Melchizedek' (Psalm 110. 4) – a priestly order of even greater antiquity and prestige than Levi's.

What shall we say, then, when in one of the twelve *Testaments* – in the *Testament of Levi* itself, no less – we find the statement that 'a king will arise out of Judah and establish a new priest-

[33] *Testament of Reuben* 6. 11 f.
[34] So in Jubilees 31. 14 f. Jacob, blessing Levi, says that his descendants 'will be princes and judges, and chiefs of all the offspring of the sons of Jacob'. The book of Jubilees is a revised edition of Genesis, composed towards the end of the second century B.C.

hood after the pattern of the Gentiles for all the Gentiles'?[35] This deviation from the normal division of the two functions between Levi and Judah goes to the opposite extreme to that which assigns kingship as well as priesthood to Levi. Here it is difficult to avoid recognising the Christian editor at work, adapting the older Jewish expectation to the circumstances of Gentile Christianity and to the portrayal in Hebrews 7. 11 of Jesus as 'another priest' of non-Levitical descent.

The Psalms of Solomon

A collection of eighteen poems from the middle of the first century B.C. has come down to us bearing the title *The Psalms of Solomon* — not that Solomon had anything to do with them, but since the canonical Old Testament Psalter was so closely associated in tradition with the name of David, perhaps the secondary status of this collection was indicated by the attachment to it of the name of his son Solomon. These psalms were composed around the time of the Roman conquest of Judaea in 63 B.C. Their original language was Hebrew, but they have been preserved in a Greek translation. The pious Jerusalem community in which they took shape looked with no kindly eye on the conquerors, impious and ruthless men as they were, but nevertheless recognised in them the instruments of divine judgment on the Hasmonaean dynasty. In this the authors of the *Psalms of Solomon* were at one with the men of Qumran, but whereas the men of Qumran saw the chief crime of the Hasmonaeans as their assumption of the high-priesthood, which belonged by right to the house of Zadok, the *Psalms of Solomon* denounce them for usurping the kingship, which belonged to the house of David, and for thus 'laying waste the throne of David'.[36] The community of these psalms placed all its hope in the speedy appearance of the long-expected son of David, who would expel the Roman oppressors and raise his people to a position of supremacy in the world.

See, O Lord, raise up for them their king, the son of David,
in the time which thou knowest, O God,

[35] *Testament of Levi* 8. 14.
[36] Psalms of Solomon 17. 8.

to reign over Israel thy servant;
and gird him with strength to shatter the unjust rulers . . .
He will possess the nations, to serve beneath his yoke;
he will glorify the Lord with the praise of all the earth.
He will cleanse Jerusalem in holiness, as it was of old,
that the nations may come from the ends of the earth to see
   his glory,
bearing as gifts her sons who had fainted,
and to see the Lord's glory with which God has glorified
   her.
A righteous king, taught by God, is their ruler,
and there will be no unrighteousness among them all his
   days;
for all will be holy, and their king is the Anointed Lord.[37]

The hope thus expressed is based on Old Testament pro-
phecies describing the latter-day glories of Israel. The closing
words, 'the Anointed Lord', are identical in Greek with those
of the angelic annunciation at Bethlehem in Luke 2. 11: 'a
Saviour, who is *Christ the Lord*' (or 'the Anointed Lord').
And in fact the *Psalms of Solomon* bring us to the eve of Luke's
nativity narrative, with its canticles so full of the same im-
minent expectation of the coming of the son of David. Thus
Gabriel speaks to Mary about her infant son in these terms
(Luke 1. 32 f.):

He will be great, and will be called the Son of the Most High;
and the Lord God will give him the throne of his father David,
and he will reign over the house of Jacob for ever;
and of his kingdom there will be no end.

The same note is struck in the hymn of Zechariah, father of
John the Baptist (Luke 1. 68 ff.):

Blessed be the Lord God of Israel,
for he has visited and redeemed his people,
and has raised up a horn of salvation for us
in the house of his servant David, . . .

[37] Psalms of Solomon 17. 23 ff.

that we should be saved from our enemies,
and from the hand of all who hate us . . .

Such were the terms in which Israel's messianic hope was voiced in the pious groups of 'the quiet in the land' into which Jesus was born.

Chapter Six

'Unwritten' Sayings and Apocryphal Gospels

Agrapha

SAYINGS or actions of Jesus not found in the authentic text of the canonical Gospels are commonly referred to as *agrapha*. This word, which means 'unwritten things', is not really appropriate, for if the *agrapha* are not written in the four Gospels, they are written elsewhere, otherwise we should not know about them.

At least one saying of Jesus, not recorded in the Gospels, is preserved elsewhere in the New Testament. In Acts 20. 35 Paul is said to have impressed on the elders of the Ephesian church their Christian duty to 'help the weak, remembering the words of the Lord Jesus, how he said, "It is more blessed to give than to receive."' And other sayings of Jesus may be present here and there in the New Testament, not so clearly identified as such.

When *agrapha* are defined as sayings (or actions) not found in the 'authentic' text of the canonical Gospels, it is implied that the term is applicable to material found in an unauthentic text. In the early Christian generations there were some 'floating' accounts of what Jesus said or did, not originally belonging to any Gospel, which were saved from being lost by being included by some scribe or editor in a manuscript of one of the Gospels. The best known instance of this is the story of Jesus's confrontation with the woman convicted of adultery, from which we get the immortal sentence: 'Let him who is without sin among you be the first to throw a stone at her.'[1] The majority of later New Testament manuscripts insert this story between John 7. 52 and 8. 12, and that is the place which it occupies in our Authorized (King James) Version. One group of manuscripts reproduces it at the end of Luke 21 (a more

[1] John 8. 7. It was the responsibility of the witnesses in an execution by stoning to throw the first stones (Deuteronomy 17. 7; cf. Acts 7. 58).

appropriate setting). But originally it formed part of neither of these Gospels.

What is called the 'Western' edition of the four Gospels and Acts of the Apostles, principally represented by a few Greek manuscripts and some copies of the older Latin version, is marked by additions to the text. Some of these can also be recognised as pieces of floating tradition, which were 'anchored' by being included in these documents. The best known of these additions comes after Luke 6. 5, immediately after the incident of Jesus and his disciples' walking in the grainfields on the sabbath day:

> The same day, seeing a certain man working on the sabbath, he said to him: 'Man, if indeed you know what you are doing, happy are you; but if not, you are accursed and a transgressor of the law.'

The implication is that a violation of the letter of the law may be permissible, and even commendable, if it is based on principle, but not if it springs from a spirit of negligence or rebellion.

Another addition follows Jesus's words in Matthew 20. 28 about his coming 'not to be served but to serve, and to give his life as a ransom for many':

> But do you seek to increase from smallness, and not from the greater to become less —

which is then amplified by the further addition of Jesus's words in Luke 14. 8–10 pointing out that it is better to take a lower place when one is guest at a feast and be invited to 'go up higher' than to take a higher place and then have to make way for someone more honourable.

One Greek manuscript of the Gospels, the fifth-century Washington Codex (so called because it belongs to the Library of Congress in Washington, D.C.), makes an interesting insertion in the longer ending of the Gospel of Mark.[2] When

[2] The original text of Mark is extant only as far as 16. 8; whether or not the clause 'for they were afraid' was designed to be the end of the Gospel is a much disputed question. There are two later endings added to the Gospel to ease the apparent abruptness with which it ends. The longer ending appears as 16. 9–20 in most of our versions; the shorter ending runs: 'But they [the women] reported briefly to Peter and those with him all that they had been told. And after this, Jesus himself sent out by means of them, from east to west, the sacred and imperishable tidings of eternal salvation.'

Jesus is said to have 'appeared to the eleven themselves as they sat at table and upbraided them for their unbelief and hardness of heart, because they had not believed those who saw him after he had risen' (Mark 16. 14), this manuscript goes on:

> And they excused themselves, saying, 'This age of lawlessness and unbelief is under Satan, who by his unclean spirits does not allow the true power of God to be comprehended. Therefore now reveal your righteousness.' So they spoke to Christ; and Christ addressed them thus: 'The limit of the years of Satan's authority has been fulfilled, but other terrible things are drawing near, even to those sinners on whose behalf I was handed over to death, that they may turn to the truth and sin no more. In order that they may inherit the spiritual and incorruptible glory of righteousness in heaven, go into all the world and preach the gospel to the whole creation' —

and so on to the end of verse 20. Jerome knew this passage as far down as the words 'Therefore now reveal your righteousness'; he had seen it in a few Greek manuscripts.[3]

Papias and Oral Tradition

Early in the second century A.D. a Christian leader in Asia Minor, Papias by name (bishop of Hierapolis in Phrygia) tells us of the pains he took to collect traditions of Jesus which might have been preserved among the disciples of those who actually heard him teach. He knew some, if not all four, of the Gospels which we have received as canonical, but he felt that a reliable oral tradition preserved a greater sense of authenticity than anything available only in written form. So, he says:

> If ever there came my way someone who had associated with the elders, I used to enquire about the words of the elders: 'What did Andrew or Peter say, or Philip or Thomas or James, or John or Matthew or any other of the Lord's disciples? What do Aristion and the elder John, the Lord's disciples, say?' For I did not suppose that what I could get from books would be so helpful to me as what came from a living and abiding voice.[4]

[3] Jerome, *Dialogue against the Pelagians* ii. 15.
[4] Quoted by Eusebius *Hist. Eccl.* iii. 39. 3 f.

Papias recorded the fruits of his research in a Greek work published in five scrolls, entitled *An Exposition of the Oracles of the Lord*. Unfortunately, this work has been lost for centuries, apart from a few extracts (like that just quoted) preserved by early Christian writers who knew it. But to judge from what survives, the information about Jesus, not available in written form, which he was able to gather from the 'living and abiding voice' did not amount to much: he evidently had to scrape the bottom of the barrel. His most famous *agraphon* describes the miraculous fruitfulness which would be enjoyed in the age to come:

The Lord taught about those times and said: 'The days will come in which vines will grow with 10,000 shoots each, and each shoot will bear 10,000 branches, each branch 10,000 twigs, each twig 10,000 clusters, each cluster 10,000 grapes, and each grape when pressed will yield twenty-five measures of wine. When any saint takes hold of one such cluster, another cluster will exclaim: "I am a better cluster; take me; bless the Lord through me!" Similarly a grain of wheat will produce 10,000 ears, each ear will have 10,000 grains, and each grain will yield ten pounds of fine flour, bright and pure; and the other fruit, seeds and herbs will be proportionately productive according to their nature, while all the animals which feed on these products of the soil will live in peace and agreement one with another, yielding complete subjection to men.'[5]

This utterance, for which Papias claimed the authority of 'John, the Lord's disciple', can be paralleled from Jewish apocalyptic literature and rabbinical tradition.[6] It is certainly consistent with the views about the glories of the resurrection age which Papias is said to have held; 'it is credible', Papias himself added, 'to those who believe'. He goes on to tell how, when Judas sceptically asked the Lord how such things could ever happen,

---

[5] Quoted by Irenaeus, *Heresies* v. 33. 3. A 'measure' of wine was equivalent to nine gallons.

[6] E.g. 2 Baruch 29. 5–8; TB *Shabbath* 30b; *Kethuboth* 111b; Midrash *Sifre* on Deuteronomy 315, 317. Cf. discussion in J. Klausner, *Jesus of Nazareth* (London, 1929), pp. 400 ff.

he was curtly told: 'Those who come to those times will see.'[7] (Judas, because of his treachery, forfeited the heritage in the resurrection age which his fellow-apostles were destined to enjoy; Papias described how he swelled up to grotesque proportions[8] before he 'burst open in the middle', as Luke tells us.)[9]

Infancy Gospels

Of the *agrapha* which have any claim at all to go back to the earliest days of Christianity, almost all have to do with what Jesus said, not with what he did. We have, to be sure, a number of 'Infancy Gospels' purporting to deal with his birth and childhood, but these are all fictitious compositions, published in order to satisfy their readers' curiosity about things on which the New Testament is silent.[10]

There is, for example, the *Protevangel of James*, which begins with an account of the birth of Mary to Joachim and Anna in their old age, when they had given up all hope of having children. Like the infant Samuel in the Old Testament, Mary was dedicated by her grateful mother to the service of God in the temple, and there she was placed in charge of the priest Zechariah. When she was twelve years old she was betrothed by her guardians to Joseph. The story of the angelic annunciation and virginal conception follows the nativity narratives of Luke and Matthew, with various embellishments: Mary's chastity is vindicated, for example, by the 'ordeal of jealousy' prescribed in Numbers 5. 11–28. In a cave near Bethlehem Mary gives birth to Jesus, Salome acting as midwife.[11] When Herod fails to find the infant, after the visit of the wise men from the east, he tries to lay hands on the child John (later the Baptist), but

---

[7] Irenaeus, *Heresies* v. 33. 4.

[8] Quoted by Apollinarius of Laodicea, as reproduced in J. A. Cramer, *Catena Graecorum Patrum in Novum Testamentum: Ad Acta SS Apostolorum* (Oxford, 1844), on Matthew 27. 5 and Acts 1. 18.

[9] Acts 1. 18.

[10] English translations of these and other uncanonical Gospels, with scholarly introductions and annotations, are provided in E. Hennecke, *New Testament Apocrypha*, English translation edited by R. McL. Wilson, Vol. 1: *Gospels and Related Writings* (London, 1963).

[11] Salome, presumably the mother of the sons of Zebedee and perhaps Mary's sister (cf. Matthew 27. 56 with Mark 15. 40 and John 19. 25), figures more prominently in uncanonical literature than she does in the New Testament (see pp. 137, 157).

when he too is not to be found (having been hidden with his mother Elizabeth in a hollow mountain) Herod has his father Zechariah put to death in the temple court.[12]

The nativity at Bethlehem and the subsequent flight of the holy family into Egypt form the theme of the *Gospel of Pseudo-Matthew*. The ox and ass worship the infant in the stable (in fulfilment of Isaiah 1. 3: 'The ox knows its owner, and the ass its master's crib'), and the wild beasts of the desert pay him homage on the way to Egypt (in fulfilment of Isaiah 11. 6 f.: 'the wolf shall dwell with the lamb, . . . and the lion shall eat straw like the ox'); while in Egypt itself three hundred and sixty-five idols fall down and are broken in pieces before him (in fulfilment of Isaiah 19. 1: 'the idols of Egypt will tremble at his presence').

Then there is the *Infancy Gospel of Thomas*,[13] which purports to describe the doings of Jesus in his boyhood. Jesus proves to be an infant prodigy at school, instructing his teachers in unsuspected mysteries of the alphabet; he astounds his family and playmates by the miracles which he performs. This is the document which tells for the first time the familiar tale of the twelve sparrows which Jesus, at the age of five, fashioned from clay on the sabbath day. Someone went and reported this to Joseph.

When Joseph came to the place and saw it, he called out to him: 'Why are you doing these things which ought not to be done on the sabbath?' But Jesus clapped his hands and called out to the sparrows: 'Be off!' And the sparrows took wing and flew away chirping.

The embellishments with which these 'Infancy Gospels' fill out the sparse details of the birth stories in Matthew and Luke are all fabricated out of whole cloth, they are not traditions of more or less dimly remembered facts; but they generated tenacious traditions of a new kind, and we shall see how greatly they have influenced the accounts of the birth of Jesus included in the Qur'ān.[14]

---

[12] This is probably a mistaken inference from Matthew 23. 35 and Luke 11. 51; the Zechariah referred to there is an Old Testament character (cf. 2 Chronicles 24. 20–22).

[13] A completely different work from the collection of sayings called the *Gospel of Thomas* which is reproduced in full in Chapter 7 below.

[14] See pp. 168 ff.

The Gospel of Peter

Towards the end of the second century Serapion, bishop of Antioch, visited the neighbouring church of Rhossus and found that it held in high esteem a Gospel bearing the name and authority of the apostle Peter. To begin with, he was not greatly concerned about this, because he believed the members of the church of Rhossus to be orthodox in their belief; but subsequent reports moved him to look into the matter more closely, and he discovered that this *Gospel of Peter* was marked by docetic teaching (from the Greek verb *dokein*, 'seem') — teaching according to which the humanity of Jesus was not real but only apparent. So he sent them a letter, part of which is quoted by Eusebius, in which he pointed out the error of the work.[15]

In 1886 there was discovered at Akhmîm in Upper Egypt (the ancient Panopolis) a small parchment codex containing (among other documents) a substantial fragment of a Greek work which is almost certainly to be identified with the *Gospel of Peter* mentioned by Eusebius. The fragment relates the passion narrative and, while it may draw in part from separate traditions, it presupposes a knowledge of all four canonical Gospels.[16] The passage immediately before the beginning of the fragment must have described Pilate's washing his hands (Matthew 27. 24), for it goes on:

> 1. But none of the Jews washed his hands, nor Herod nor any of his judges. Since they refused to wash, Pilate rose up [i.e. ended the trial]. Then King Herod commanded the Lord to be taken away, saying to them: 'Do all that I have commanded you to do to him.'

[15] Eusebius, *Hist. Eccl.* vi. 12. 2–6. Origen (*Commentary on Matthew* 10. 17) says that the *Gospel of Peter* was invoked by those who held that Jesus's brothers and sisters, mentioned in the Gospels, were children of Joseph by an earlier wife than Mary, and elsewhere he shows acquaintance with elements found in the *Gospel of Peter*.

[16] From Matthew, e.g., come Pilate's hand-washing, the mingling of 'gall' with the drink given to the crucified Jesus, the earthquake and the watch at the tomb; from Mark comes the appearance of the 'young man' to the women at the tomb and the identification of Levi as the 'son of Alphaeus'; from Luke come the involvement of Herod Antipas in the trial of Jesus, the incident of the penitent robber and the breast-beating of the spectators at Jesus's death; from John come the nails and the leg-breaking, and the disciples' return to their fishing.

2. There stood there Joseph, the friend of Pilate and of the Lord, and knowing that they were going to crucify him, he went to Pilate and asked that he might have the Lord's body for burial. Pilate sent to Herod and asked for his body, and Herod said: 'Brother Pilate, even if no one had asked for him, we should have buried him, since the sabbath is drawing on. For it is written in the law that the sun must not set on one who has been put to death.'[17]

3. So he handed him over to the people before the first day of unleavened bread, their festival. They took the Lord and ran, pushing him and saying: 'Let us drag the son of God, now that we have got him into our power.' They clothed him in purple, and made him sit on a judgment-seat,[18] saying: 'Judge righteously, king of Israel!' One of them brought a crown of thorns and placed it on the Lord's head; others standing by spat in his eyes, and other struck his cheeks. Yet others pricked him with a reed, and some flogged him, saying: 'This is the honour with which we honour the son of God.'

4. Then they brought two criminals and crucified the Lord between them. But he remained silent, as though he felt no pain. When they had raised up the cross, they wrote on it an inscription: 'This is the King of Israel.' Laying his clothes in front of them, they shared them out, and cast lots for them. One of those criminals reproached them, saying: 'We have suffered thus because of the crimes we have committed, but as for this man, the saviour of men, what harm has he done you?' They were annoyed at him, and ordered that his legs should not be broken, so that he might die in agony.[19]

5. Now it was midday, and darkness covered all Judaea. They were troubled and distressed, lest the sun should have set while he was still alive. (For it is written that the sun must not set on one who has been put to death.) One of them said: 'Give him gall with vinegar to drink.'[20] So they made the

[17] Deuteronomy 21. 23 (cf. John 19. 31).
[18] This might arise from a misunderstanding of John 19. 13, where *Pilate* sits on the judgment-seat. Similarly Justin Martyr (*First Apology* 35. 6) says that, 'as the prophet said, they dragged him off and made him sit on the judgment-seat and said, "Execute judgment for us" ' – 'the prophet' being a reference to Isaiah 58. 2: 'they ask of me righteous judgments'.
[19] The breaking of the legs of crucified men was designed to hasten death.
[20] In fulfilment of Psalm 69. 21 (cf. Matthew 27. 34, where 'gall' corresponds to the stupefacient 'myrrh' of Mark 15. 23).

mixture and gave it to him to drink. Thus they fulfilled everything, and completed the tale of their sins on their own heads. Many went about with lamps, thinking that it was night [and some] fell down. Then the Lord cried out: 'My power, my power, you have left me!' So saying, he was taken up. The same hour the curtain of the sanctuary in Jerusalem was torn in two.

6. Then they drew out the nails from the Lord's hands and laid him on the ground. The whole earth quaked and great fear fell on them. Then the sun shone out and it was found to be the ninth hour (3 p.m.). The Jews rejoiced, and gave his body to Joseph to be buried, since he had beheld all the good things he had done. So, taking the Lord, he washed him, wrapped him in linen and brought him into his own tomb, called Joseph's Garden.

7. Then the Jews and the elders and priests, realising what harm they had done themselves, began to beat their breasts[21] and say: 'Alas for our sins! The judgment and end of Jerusalem has drawn near.' But I [Peter], with my companions, was grief-stricken; wounded in mind we hid ourselves, for they were searching for us as men that were criminals, who wished to set the sanctuary on fire. Over and above all this we fasted, and sat mourning and weeping night and day until the sabbath.[22]

8. The scribes, Pharisees and elders came together, for they heard that all the people were murmuring and beating their breasts and saying: 'If these stupendous signs have happened at his death, see what a righteous man he must have been.' The elders were afraid, and they came to Pilate with a request: 'Give us soldiers so that we may guard his sepulchre for three days, lest his disciples come and steal him and the people suppose that he has risen from the dead and do us harm.' Pilate gave them Petronius the centurion with soldiers to guard the tomb. The elders and scribes came to the sepulchre with them, and all who were there together rolled a great stone and placed it at the door of the sepulchre, [as a

[21] Cf. Luke 23. 48.

[22] The mourning and weeping night and day are envisaged as beginning on the night of Jesus's arrest. The sequel makes it plain that in this record, as in the canonical Gospels, the crucifixion took place the day before the sabbath.

precaution] against the centurion and the soldiers, and fixed seven seals on it. Then, pitching a tent there, they guarded it. Early in the morning, as the sabbath was dawning, a crowd came from Jerusalem and the surrounding area to see the sealed sepulchre.

9. On the night when the Lord's day[23] was drawing on, while the soldiers were keeping watch two at a time, a great voice sounded in heaven and they saw the heavens opened and two men descend thence, with a great light, and draw near to the tomb. That stone which had been laid at the door rolled away of its own accord and allowed partial access; the tomb was opened and both the young men went in. When those soldiers saw this, they roused the centurion and the elders from sleep (for the elders were also present on guard). They described what they had seen, and then three men were seen leaving the tomb, the [first] two supporting the other, and a cross was seen following them. The heads of the two reached up to heaven, but the head of him whom they led by the hand reached above the heavens. They heard a voice from the heavens saying: 'Have you preached to those who sleep?' And from the cross was heard an answer: 'Yes!'

10. So those men conferred and decided to go and report these things to Pilate. While they were still pondering it in their minds, they saw the heavens opened again and a man descend and enter into the sepulchre. When the centurion and his men saw this they made haste to Pilate while it was still night, leaving the tomb which they were guarding, and they related all that they had seen, greatly agitated and saying: 'Truly he was God's Son.' Pilate replied: 'I am clean from the blood of God's Son; this was your decision.'[24] Then they all came and begged and besought him to command the centurion and soldiers not to tell anything that they had seen. 'It is more expedient', they said, 'that we should incur the utmost guilt in God's sight than that we should fall into the hands of the Jewish people and be stoned.' So Pilate commanded the centurion and soldiers not to say anything.

---

[23] That is, Sunday ('the first day of the week' in the New Testament resurrection narratives).

[24] In Matthew 27. 24 Pilate's protestation of innocence accompanies his hand-washing.

11. At dawn on the Lord's day Mary Magdalene, a disciple of the Lord, took her friends with her and came to the sepulchre where he had been laid. (She had not previously performed at the Lord's sepulchre the services customarily performed by women for the dead and for those whom they love, through fear of the Jews, for they were inflamed with anger.) They were afraid lest the Jews might see them, but they said: 'Even if we were unable to weep and beat our breasts on the day when he was crucified, now let us do these things at his sepulchre. But who will roll us away the stone which has been placed at the door of the sepulchre, that we may go in and sit down and perform what is proper? The stone was a great one, and we are afraid someone will see us. But even if we cannot do so, if we lay what we have brought for his memorial at the door, we will weep and beat our breasts and then go home.' So they set out and found the tomb opened. Drawing near, they bent down and looked in there, and there they saw a beautiful young man sitting in the centre of the tomb, dressed in a shining robe.[25] He said to them: 'Why have you come? Whom do you seek? Not him who was crucified? He has risen and gone away. If you do not believe, bend down and look in and see the place where he lay, for he is not there. He has risen and gone away to the place from which he was sent.' Then the women feared and fled.[26]

12. Now it was the last day of unleavened bread, and many people were going out [from Jerusalem] and returning home, because the festival had come to an end. But we, the twelve disciples of the Lord, wept and mourned, and each went off to his home mourning because of what had happened. But I, Simon Peter, and Andrew my brother took our nets and set out for the sea.[27] With us was Levi the son of Alphaeus,[28] whom the Lord . . .

---

[25] This is based on Mark 16. 5: 'a young man . . . dressed in a white robe'.

[26] This is another instance of Markan influence: Mark's extant record breaks off at 16. 8 with the women's panic-stricken flight from the tomb (cf. p. 83, n. 2).

[27] Cf. John 21. 3.

[28] Only in Mark 2. 14 is Levi (mentioned without patronymic in Luke 5. 27) called 'the son of Alphaeus'. He is not listed as a member of the fishing expedition in John 21. 2.

Here the fragment breaks off, but the last sentence probably went on: 'whom the Lord had called from the tax office' (Mark 2. 14). Then presumably came the account of the risen Lord's appearance to them, perhaps along the lines of the narrative in John 21.

The docetic note in this narrative appears in the statement that Jesus, while being crucified, 'remained silent, as though he felt no pain', and in the account of his death. It carefully avoids saying that he died, preferring to say that he 'was taken up', as though he — or at least his soul or spiritual self — was 'assumed' direct from the cross to the presence of God.[29] (We shall see an echo of this idea in the Qur'ān.)[30] Then the cry of dereliction is reproduced in a form which suggests that, at that moment, his divine power[31] left the bodily shell in which it had taken up temporary residence.

Apart from its docetic tendency, the most striking feature of the narrative is its complete exoneration of Pilate from all responsibility for the crucifixion of Jesus. Pilate is here well on the way to the goal of canonisation which he was to attain in the Coptic Church. He withdraws from the trial after washing his hands, and Herod Antipas takes over from him, assuming the responsibility which, in Luke's passion narrative, he declined to accept. Roman soldiers play no part until they are sent by Pilate, at the request of the Jewish authorities, to provide the guard at the tomb of Jesus. The villains of the piece throughout are 'the Jews' — more particularly, the chief priests and the scribes. It is they who condemn Jesus to death and abuse him; it is they who crucify him and share out his clothes among themselves. Unhistorical as this representation is, it became a widely accepted tradition, calling for repudiation as recently as Vatican Council II, and (like the docetism) influencing the Islamic account of the passion.[32]

The Gospel of Nicodemus

The question addressed from heaven to the risen Lord,

[29] The expression, to be 'taken up', is used of Jesus in Luke 9. 51 and Acts 1. 2, but not so as to exclude the idea of his dying.

[30] See p. 174.

[31] Behind the repeated words 'my power' may lie some awareness that the root meaning of Hebrew *'el* ('God'), found in the suffixed form *'eli* ('my God') in Psalm 22. 1 and so quoted in Matthew 27. 46, is 'power'.

[32] See pp. 175 f.

'Have you preached to those who are asleep?' is probably based on the Petrine literature in the New Testament — on 1 Peter 3. 18–20, where Christ, 'put to death in the flesh but made alive in the spirit', is said to have gone and preached to the imprisoned spirits who were disobedient in Noah's day,[33] and 1 Peter 4. 6, where the gospel is said to have been 'preached even to the dead, that though judged in the flesh like men, they might live in the spirit like God'. Such passages were greatly elaborated in the later motif of Christ's 'harrowing of hell', in which his invasion of the realm of the dead is portrayed after the fashion of Greek heroes like Theseus, Heracles and Orpheus who entered the underworld to defy its rulers or rescue its victims. The earliest literary form of this motif is appended to the work alternatively called the *Gospel of Nicodemus* or the *Acts of Pilate*. Mention has been made in an earlier chapter of the 'Acts of Pilate' published in A.D. 311 by the Emperor Maximinus II to serve as antichristian propaganda. The Christian *Acts of Pilate* which has come down to us from the fourth century may have been published as a counterblast to this propaganda, but there is reason to think that its core goes back to the second century.[34]

The main part of the Christian *Acts of Pilate* presents an expanded version of the trial and death of Jesus, based mainly on the narratives in Matthew and John. When Jesus is brought in before Pilate, the imperial images on the military standards bowed down and paid him homage. (Historically, indeed, out of deference to Jewish scruples and the status of Jerusalem as a holy city, the images surmounting the Roman standards were left outside the city when the military units to which they belonged entered,[35] but this state of affairs came to an end in A.D. 70, and the author may not have known of it, even if he had any concern for historical accuracy.) Then, as soon as Jesus took his position before Pilate, Pilate received the warning message from his wife, recorded in Matthew 27. 19,

[33] In fact, those spirits were not the spirits of men but fallen angels — the 'sons of God' who, according to Genesis 6. 1–4, were captivated by the beauty of the 'daughters of men'.

[34] It may have been known to Justin and Tertullian; see E. Hennecke, *New Testament Apocrypha*, Vol. 1, pp. 444–7 (Lutterworth Press, 1963).

[35] Pilate actually got into trouble when he insisted on bringing them inside the walls (Josephus, *War* ii. 169–74; *Antiquities* xviii. 55–59).

and Pilate called all the Jews to him and said to them: 'You know that my wife is a God-fearer[36] and prefers Jewish ways, like yours.' 'Yes', said they, 'we know.' 'See', said Pilate to them, 'my wife has sent me a message: "Have nothing to do with that righteous man, for I have suffered much over him last night."' 'Did we not tell you that he was a sorcerer?' they replied. 'See, he has sent your wife a nightmare.'

Then one witness after another comes forward to testify in Jesus's defence[37] – Nicodemus; the man whom Jesus healed of a paralysis which had lasted thirty-eight years ('Aha', said the accusers, 'but it was the sabbath day when he did it!');[38] blind Bartimaeus, whose sight he restored;[39] the bent man whom he straightened;[40] the leper whom he cleansed,[41] and Bernice (Veronica), whose haemorrhage ceased when she touched the hem of his garment[42] ('Our law', they protested, 'does not admit a woman's evidence'). But all this favourable testimony is in vain; the popular clamour demands Jesus's death, and Pilate gives in to it. (His exoneration has not proceeded so far in this work as in the *Gospel of Peter*.) He orders Jesus to be crucified in the garden where he was arrested.[43]

Here the two criminals who were crucified with Jesus receive their traditional names, Dysmas (who received the assurance of Paradise) and Gestas.[44] The circumstances of Jesus's death are reported to Pilate by the centurion.

And when the governor and his wife heard it, they were greatly grieved, and neither ate nor drank that day. Then

---

[36] That is, a Gentile attached in some degree to the Jewish religion without being a full convert or proselyte. Josephus uses the same word of Nero's wife Poppaea (*Antiquities* xx. 195). On Pilate's wife cf. p. 45 with n. 7.

[37] Curiously, the first question to be investigated in Pilate's court according to this account concerned the legitimacy of Jesus's birth (cf. pp. 57, 150 f., 175).

[38] The incidents of Mark 2. 2–12 and John 5. 2–15 are here conflated.

[39] Mark 10. 46 ff.

[40] In Luke 13. 10–17 this is related of a woman, not of a man.

[41] Mark 1. 40–44.

[42] Mark 8. 43–48. She is not named in the New Testament.

[43] This is a confusion of the two quite distinct gardens of John 18. 1 and 19. 41.

[44] The soldier who pierced Jesus's side is also named as Longinus (16. 7).

Pilate sent for the Jews and said to them: 'Have you seen what has happened?' But they said: 'It was an ordinary eclipse of the sun.'[45]

Pilate plays no further part, but Nicodemus continues as chief narrator. Joseph of Arimathaea is arrested and sentenced to death by the Jewish authorities for paying the last respects to the body of Jesus, but when he is sought for execution on the morning after the sabbath, he is not to be found in his cell — to the consternation of all, 'because the seals were found intact and Caiaphas had the key'. Later, Joseph reveals that the newly risen Jesus appeared to him in his cell, and transferred him to his own house in Arimathaea. By this time Annas, Caiaphas and their associates are more than a little shaken, and are almost persuaded to believe in Jesus's claims, especially when three messengers arrive from Galilee and bear witness separately to the circumstances of Jesus's ascension. The priests and Levites agree that if Jesus is still remembered after a jubilee (50 years) has elapsed, 'he will have dominion for ever and will raise up for himself a new people'.

When Matthew records the death of Jesus and the tearing of the temple curtain, he makes a strange addition not found in any other Gospel: 'the tombs also were opened, and many bodies of the saints which had fallen asleep were raised, and coming out of the tombs after his resurrection they went into the holy city and appeared to many' (27. 52 f.).

This enigmatic passage invited imaginative expansion, such as we find in an appendix to the *Gospel of Nicodemus*. According to this appendix the saints who emerged from their tombs included Simeon of Jerusalem, who once held the infant Jesus in his arms (Luke 2. 25–35), and his two sons, who had recently died and been buried. The two sons were brought before the chief priests in Jerusalem and adjured to tell how they had been raised from the dead. They asked for writing materials and wrote down their testimony.

The midnight darkness in Hades, they said, was suddenly dispersed by a great light, in which the prophet Isaiah, who was there with 'all those who had fallen asleep from ages past', recognised the fulfilment of his own words: 'The people that

[45] See p. 30.

96

sat in darkness have seen a great light' (Isaiah 9. 2). Then John the Baptist rose and called on all who had been idolaters on earth to seize the present unrepeatable opportunity and worship the one who was about to enter, whom in his lifetime he had acclaimed as 'the Lamb of God, who takes away the sin of the world' (John 1. 29). After him Adam bade his son Seth tell them all the message he had received when he was sent to the gate of Paradise to beg some oil from the tree of life to anoint his father in his mortal sickness. 'After I had prayed', Seth told them:

the angel of the Lord said to me: 'What do you want, Seth? The oil which raises up the sick, or the tree which flows with such oil, for your father's sickness? This is not now to be found. Go then and tell your father that when 5,500 years have been completed from the creation of the world,[46] the only Son of God, having become man, will descend into the earth, and he will anoint him with such oil; then he will rise and wash him and his descendants with water and the Holy Spirit, and he will be healed from every disease. But at present this is impossible.'

Seth's story filled all the patriarchs and prophets with joy: now the time of their release was at hand.

Meanwhile Satan and Hades (the personified lord of the realm of death) hold agitated debate about what they should do. Satan wants Hades to seize Jesus and bind him fast the moment he sets foot in his realm; but Hades, remembering how not long before Jesus had snatched Lazarus from his grasp, has no hope of being able to hold Jesus himself. While they are still arguing, a voice like thunder is heard: 'Lift up your gates, O rulers![47] Be lifted up, O eternal doors, and the King of glory will come in' (Psalm 24. 7). Satan and Hades talk ineffectively of barring the invader's path, but David tells them that he himself foretold this challenge when he lived on earth, while Isaiah adds that he too, by the Holy Spirit, prophesied: 'The dead shall rise; those

[46] Calculations based on the Hebrew text of the Old Testament make the interval from Adam to Christ 4,000 years, but the calculation here is based on the Greek (Septuagint) version, in which the chronology is expanded.

[47] This is the Greek (Septuagint) rendering; the Hebrew text, of course, has 'Lift up your heads, O gates!'

who are in the tombs shall be raised up, and those who are in the earth shall rejoice' (Isaiah 25. 8). Again the challenge is sounded, and when Hades—'as if he did not know, forsooth'—asks 'Who is this King of glory?' he not only receives the inevitable answer in word ('The Lord strong and mighty, the Lord mighty in battle') but a matching answer in deed:

> Immediately, with this word, the gates of bronze were broken in pieces, the bars of iron were smashed, and all the dead who were bound were set free from their chains, and we with them. Then the King of glory entered in human form, and all the dark places of Hades were illuminated.

Jesus then blessed Adam and the other righteous dead with the sign of the cross on their foreheads and led them out of Hades.

> So he went into Paradise leading our first father Adam by the hand, and entrusted him, with all the righteous, to the care of Michael the archangel. As they went in by the door of Paradise, there met them two aged men, to whom the holy fathers said: 'Who are you, that you did not see death or go down into Hades, but have been dwelling in Paradise, body and soul together?' One of them answered: 'I am Enoch, who pleased God and was translated here by him, and this is Elijah the Tishbite. We are to live until the close of the age. Then we shall be sent by God when Antichrist arises, and we shall be killed by him, but after three days we shall rise again and be caught up in clouds to meet the Lord.'[48]
>
> While they were saying this, another came up, a humble man, carrying a cross on his shoulders. The holy fathers said to him: 'Who are you with the appearance of a robber, and what is the cross you are carrying on your shoulders?' 'I was indeed, as you say, a robber and a thief in the world', he replied, 'and therefore the Jews arrested me and delivered me to the cross along with our Lord Jesus Christ. While he was hanging on the cross, I believed in him, seeing the signs

[48] Enoch and Elijah are here identified as the 'two witnesses' whose ministry, martyrdom, resurrection and ascension are described in Revelation 11. 3–12. The final words, 'to meet the Lord', are derived from 1 Thessalonians 4. 17.

which took place. Then I entreated him: "Lord, when you become king, do not forget me." Immediately he said to me: "Indeed and in truth, today, I tell you, you will be with me in Paradise."[49] So I came into Paradise still carrying my cross, and finding the archangel Michael I said to him: "Our Lord Jesus, the Crucified One, has sent me here. Bring me therefore to the gate of Eden." When the flaming sword saw the sign of the cross, it opened to me and I entered in.[50] Then the archangel said to me: "Wait a little, because Adam, the first father of the human race, is coming with the righteous, that they too may enter in." And now, seeing you, I have come to meet you.'

Having written their testimony and concluded it with the apostolic benediction,[51] the two brothers sealed the scrolls, gave half to the chief priests and half to Joseph and Nicodemus, and disappeared from their sight.

The Gospel according to the Hebrews

From this dramatic portrayal of the truth that Christ 'abolished death and brought life and immortality to death through the gospel' (2 Timothy 1. 10) we return to a document in somewhat closer touch with the historical Jesus. This is the *Gospel according to the Hebrews*. This appears to have been a paraphrase of the Gospel of Matthew, partly amplified and partly abridged,[52] the text of which was preserved at Caesarea and was known to Origen (*c*. A.D. 231) and Eusebius (*c*. A.D. 325). According to Eusebius it was known to Hegesippus (*c*. A.D. 170).[53] An unsolved problem is the relation of this work to an Aramaic Gospel which Jerome found in use among the Nazarenes (orthodox Jewish Christians) of Beroea (Aleppo) in Syria and which he claims to have translated into Greek and Latin, under the impression that it was the Aramaic original of the Gospel of Matthew. The copy at Beroea, he says, was made

[49] Cf. Luke 23. 43.
[50] The 'flaming sword' was stationed at the east of Eden 'to guard the way to the tree of life' (Genesis 3. 24).
[51] 2 Corinthians 13. 14.
[52] According to the ninth-century *Stichometry* of Nicephorus the *Gospel according to the Hebrews* consisted of 2200 lines as against Matthew's 2500.
[53] Eusebius, *Hist. Eccl.* iv. 22. 8.

from a master-copy, 'the Hebrew text', in the library founded at Caesarea by Pamphilus, the teacher of Eusebius.[54] The work which Jerome translated may have been an Aramaic version of the *Gospel according to the Hebrews* or it may have been a separate Jewish-Christian compilation, bearing some relation to the Gospel of Matthew.

In reproducing below the principal extracts quoted in the works of Origen, Eusebius and Jerome[55] from the *Gospel according to the Hebrews* or the *Nazarene Gospel* (for which the order of the Gospel of Matthew is followed as far as possible), we make no assumption about their identity or independence, since the evidence one way or the other is not conclusive.

> *1.* '*Let us go and be baptised*' (*cf. Matthew 3. 13–15*)
> Behold, the mother of the Lord and his brothers said to him: 'John the Baptist is baptising for the remission of sins; let us go and be baptised by him.' But he said to them: 'What sin have I committed, that I should go and be baptised by him? — unless perchance this very thing that I have said is a sin of ignorance.'

That Jesus, who was sinless, should submit to a 'baptism of repentance for the remission of sins' constituted a problem which called for comment. According to Matthew, John demurred at Jesus's request to be baptised;[56] here Jesus himself demurs at his family's proposal that he should join them in seeking baptism at John's hands. Jerome quotes this extract from 'the *Gospel according to the Hebrews* in Chaldaean and Syriac speech [i.e. Aramaic], written in Hebrew letters, which the Nazarenes use, also called [the Gospel] according to the Apostles or according to Matthew, which is to be seen in the library at Caesarea'.[57]

> *2. After the baptism* (*cf. Matthew 3. 16 f.*)

[54] Jerome, *On illustrious men* 3; *Commentary on Matthew* 12. 13. It has been pointed out that he ceases to make this claim after he wrote his *Commentary on Matthew* (A.D. 401); probably the detailed study of Matthew convinced him that this could not be its (hypothetical) Aramaic original.

[55] For a quotation from this Gospel by Clement of Alexandria see p. 113 with n. 9.

[56] Matthew 3. 14.

[57] *Against the Pelagians* iii. 2.

Now it happened that, when the Lord had come up out of the water, the whole fountain of the Holy Spirit came down and rested on him, and said to him: 'My son, in all the prophets I was waiting for you to come that I might rest in you. For you are my rest, you are my first-begotten Son, reigning as king for ever.'

This bears the marks of a *targum* or expanded paraphrase of the canonical account of the descent of the Spirit and the heavenly voice at Jesus's baptism. It reflects the words about the coming 'shoot from the stump of Jesse' in Isaiah 11. 2: 'the Spirit of the Lord shall rest upon him'. It is quoted by Jerome from 'the Gospel in the Hebrew speech, which the Nazarenes use'.[58]

3. 'My mother the Holy Spirit' (cf. Matthew 4. 1f)

But now my mother the Holy Spirit took me by one of my hairs and carried me off to the great mountain Tabor.

This is quoted from the *Gospel according to the Hebrews* both by Origen and by Jerome.[59] It is apparently a counterpart to the beginning of the temptation story, according to which 'Jesus was led up by the Spirit into the wilderness to be tempted by the devil' (compare the 'very high mountain' of Matthew 4. 8), but the reference to Mount Tabor is strange: Tabor is traditionally the 'high mountain' of the transfiguration narrative (Matthew 17. 1). A Semitic origin for this saying is practically certain, since the word for 'Spirit' in the Semitic languages is feminine (whereas it is neuter in Greek and masculine in Latin); hence only in a Semitic context was it linguistically natural to treat the Holy Spirit as Jesus's mother.

4. The plea of the man with the withered hand (cf. Matthew 12. 10)

'I was a stonemason, earning my living with my hands. I

---

[58] *Commentary on Isaiah* 11. 2.

[59] Origen, *Commentary on John* 2. 6; *Homilies on Jeremiah* 15. 4; Jerome, *Commentary on Micah* 7. 6. In the first-named place Origen says there is no difficulty in the wording: 'if he who does the will of the Father in heaven is Christ's brother and sister and mother (Matthew 12. 50), . . . then there is nothing absurd in the Holy Spirit's being his mother, every one being his mother who does the will of the Father in heaven.'

pray you, Jesus, restore my health to me, so that I may not be shamefully reduced to begging my food.'

Jerome quotes this from 'the Gospel which the Nazarenes and Ebionites use, and which many regard as the original of Matthew'.[60] With this man's elaboration of his plight we may compare the leper's explanation of how he contracted his disease in Egerton Papyrus 2.[61]

5. How often shall I forgive? (cf. Matthew 18. 15–22)

(a) 'If your brother sins in word and makes amends to you, receive him', said he, 'seven times a day.' His disciple Simon said to him: 'Seven times a day?' The Lord replied: 'Yes, I tell you, and seventy times seven; for even in the prophets, after they were anointed with the Holy Spirit, sinful language was found.'

Jerome quotes this from 'the same book' as the discussion between Jesus and his family about submitting to John's baptism.[62] The reference to 'sinful language' in the prophets may have in mind Moses, who under provocation 'spoke words that were rash' (Psalm 106. 33).

(b) And never be joyful, unless you look on your brother in love.

In commenting on Ephesians 5. 4 Jerome quotes this extract from the 'Hebrew Gospel'.

(c) It is included among the greatest sins for a man to grieve his brother's spirit.

This sentiment, which is quite similar to the preceding one, is said by Jerome to be found in 'the Gospel according to the Hebrews which the Nazarenes use';[63] it is not a direct quotation, but a summary in Jerome's own words. Cf. Ephesians

[60] *Commentary on Matthew* 12. 13.
[61] See p. 162.
[62] *Against the Pelagians* iii. 2.
[63] *Commentary on Ezekiel* 18. 7.

4. 30: 'do not grieve the Holy Spirit of God' (primarily, as the context indicates, in one's fellows).

6. A rich man and the way to eternal life (cf. Matthew 19. 16–22)

The other rich man said to him: 'Master, what good thing shall I do in order to have life?' He said to him: 'Man, keep the law and the prophets.' 'I have kept them', was his reply. He said to him: 'Go, sell all that you possess and share it out among the poor and come, follow me.' Then the rich man began to scratch his head: he did not like it. The Lord said to him: 'How can you say, "I have kept the law and the prophets"? It is written in the law: "You shall love your neighbour as yourself" – and look, many of your brothers, sons of Abraham, are dressed in filthy rags and dying of hunger, while your house is full of many good things, yet nothing at all goes forth from it to them.' Then he turned and said to his disciple Simon who was sitting beside him: 'Simon, son of John, it is easier for a camel to enter in through a needle's eye than for a rich man to enter into the kingdom of heaven.'

Although this incident, inserted by the Latin translator into Origen's commentary on Matthew,[64] ostensibly concerns another rich man than the one mentioned in the canonical record, it is essentially an expansion of the canonical account of the rich young man.[65]

7. The three servants and the talents (cf. Matthew 25. 14–30)

The master left behind three servants. One of them greatly multiplied his stock-in-trade; one hid his talent, and one consumed his master's property with harlots and flute-girls. The first was warmly greeted, the second was reprehended, but the third was thrown into prison.

This summary of a more diversified rendering of the parable of the talents is said by Eusebius to come from 'the Gospel written in Hebrew characters which has reached our hands', in

---

[64] Pseudo-Origen (Latin), Commentary on Matthew 15. 14.
[65] See p. 165 for an expansion of the Markan parallel.

which, he continues, the severest penalty was imposed 'not on him who hid his talent but on him who indulged in riotous living'.[66]

8. The lintel of the temple (cf. Matthew 27. 51)
The lintel of the temple, which was of immense size, was cracked in two.

According to Jerome, this statement in 'the Gospel written in Hebrew letters' replaced the canonical statement that 'the curtain of the temple was torn in two, from top to bottom'.[67] Perhaps the cracking of the lintel seemed a more natural consequence of the earthquake which Matthew describes at that moment, and Old Testament precedents may have been recognised in Isaiah 6. 4 and Amos 9. 1.

9. An appearance of the risen Christ
When he came to Peter and his companions, he said to them: 'Take hold, feel me and see that I am not a bodiless spirit.' Immediately they touched him and believed . . .

This is a parallel not to anything in the Gospel of Matthew but to Luke 24. 39, where the risen Christ appears to 'the eleven' and calms their startled apprehensions with the invitation: 'handle me, and see; for a spirit has not flesh and bones as you see that I have'. The other version, reproduced above, comes from Ignatius's *Letter to the Smyrnaeans* (c. A.D. 110)[68] and might simply be an instance of free quotation or quotation from memory; but Jerome says that the words were taken 'from the Gospel which was lately translated by me'.[69] It would be surprising if the *Gospel according to the Hebrews* (or whatever document Jerome translated) should be dated as early as the time of Ignatius.

10. 'He appeared to James'

---

[66] Eusebius, *Theophania* (Syriac) iv. 12. The lesson of this parable is inculcated also by the *agraphon* 'Become approved money-changers', frequently quoted by Origen (e.g. on Ephesians 4. 25a) and after him by Jerome (e.g. on Ephesians 4. 31 f.).

[67] *Commentary on Matthew* 27. 51; *Epistles* 120. 8 (to Hedibia).

[68] Ignatius, *Smyrnaeans* 3. 2.

[69] Jerome, *On illustrious men* 16.

Now when the Lord had given his linen garment to the priest's servant, he went to James and appeared to him. For James had sworn that he would eat no bread from that hour when he had drunk the cup of the Lord until he saw him rising from the dead. [And again, a little later:] 'Bring a table and bread', said the Lord; [and immediately it continues:] He took bread and gave thanks and broke it, and thereafter he gave it to James the Just and said to him: 'My brother, eat your bread, because the Son of Man has risen from those who sleep.'

None of the canonical Gospels records that the risen Christ appeared to James. Paul briefly states that he did so (1 Corinthians 15. 7), having probably received the information from James himself (cf. Galatians 1. 19, where Paul mentions that he met 'James the Lord's brother' in Jerusalem in the third year after his conversion). If we had no reference at all to such an appearance to James, we should be compelled to postulate that something of the sort took place: otherwise it would be difficult to understand how James and other members of the holy family, who remained aloof from Jesus during his Palestinian ministry, came to be closely and prominently associated with his followers after his death and resurrection. Jerome says he derived this account of the appearance to James from 'the Gospel which is called "according to the Hebrews" and was lately translated by me into the Greek and Latin speech, of which Origen also frequently makes use'.[70]

The Ebionite Gospel

Another edited text of the Gospel of Matthew was in use among the Ebionites, an important Jewish-Christian community in Transjordan and the neighbouring territories who, unlike Jerome's friends the Nazarenes of Beroea, were not orthodox according to the beliefs and practices of what had become main-line catholic Christianity, but deviated from them in several respects. Our chief informant about this edition is Epiphanius, bishop of Salamis in Cyprus (c. A.D. 375); but it has sometimes been thought that Origen and Jerome also mention it under the title the *Gospel according to the Twelve* or

[70] *On illustrious men* 2.

the *Gospel according to the Apostles*:[71] this may be so, but we cannot be sure. According to Epiphanius, it was the only Gospel accepted by the Ebionites, and they called it the 'Gospel according to the Hebrews'.[72] The Ebionites are said to have denied the virgin birth of Jesus and to have held that his divine sonship dated from his baptism, when the Holy Spirit entered into union with him. Accordingly, their Gospel omitted the nativity narrative,[73] and began thus:

> It happened in the days of Herod, king of Judaea, that John came baptising with a baptism of repentance in the River Jordan. He was said to be of the family of Aaron the priest, the son of Zechariah and Elizabeth. All went out to him.[74]

The note about John's descent and parentage is derived not from Matthew but from Luke 1. 5 ff.

Further details about John are given as follows:

> John came baptising, and Pharisees went out to him and were baptised, and so did all Jerusalem. John had a garment of camel's hair and wore a girdle of skin round his waist, and his food was wild honey, with the taste of manna, like a cake dipped in olive oil.[75]

The manna in the Old Testament narrative tasted 'like wafers made with honey' (Exodus 16. 31); here the comparison is reversed. John, incidentally, becomes a vegetarian by the change of *akris*, the Greek word for 'locust' (Matthew 3. 4), to *enkris*, meaning 'cake'. We shall find other instances of a similar

[71] See p. 100.

[72] Epiphanius, *Heresies* 30. 13.

[73] An anti-Jewish counterpart is provided by Marcion's Gospel, an edition of Luke which omitted the nativity narrative and began with Luke 3. 1a followed immediately by 4. 31: 'In the fifteenth year of the reign of Tiberius, Jesus came down to Capernaum, a city of Galilee' (Tertullian, *Against Marcion* iv. 7).

[74] Epiphanius, *Heresies* 30. 13 f. If we are to exonerate the author from a gross anachronism (since Herod, king of Judaea, died in 4 B.C. and John's ministry began in A.D. 27/28), we shall have to suppose that Herod, tetrarch of Galilee is meant, but if so, the title is inaccurate. After the reference to Herod the words 'in the high-priesthood of Caiaphas' may have been added (cf. Luke 3. 2).

[75] Epiphanius, *Heresies* 30. 13.

change, made for dogmatic reasons, in the canonical account of John's diet.[76] Since the play on the similar-sounding words for 'locust' and 'cake' is possible only in Greek, it may be inferred that the *Ebionite Gospel* was a Greek one.

John's baptism of Jesus is recorded thus:

> When the people had been baptised, Jesus also came and was baptised by John. When he came up from the water, the heavens were opened and he saw the Holy Spirit coming down in the form of a dove and entering into him. A voice from heaven was heard: 'You are my beloved Son; in you I am well pleased.' And again: 'Today I have begotten you.' Immediately a great light shone round about the place. When John saw this, he said to him: 'Who are you?' And again a voice from heaven said to John: 'This is my beloved Son, in whom I am well pleased.' Then John fell at his feet and said: 'I pray you, Lord, do you baptise me.' But he forbade him, saying: 'Let it be: thus it is fitting that all things should be fulfilled.'[77]

The narrative is based for the most part on Matthew, but the heavenly voice speaks twice, first addressing Jesus in the language of Mark 1. 11 and the Western text of Luke 3. 22 — 'Today I have begotten you' (from Psalm 2. 7) — and then addressing John in the language of Matthew 3. 17. The Holy Spirit does not merely alight on Jesus (as in Matthew 3. 16) but enters into him, and John's demurrer at the idea of his baptising Jesus comes later than in Matthew (after Jesus receives the divine nature). The light which shone around at Jesus's baptism is mentioned in a couple of Old Latin Gospel texts at Matthew 3. 11, and also in Tatian's *Diatessaron* or harmony of the four Gospels, compiled about A.D. 170.[78]

The call of Jesus's disciples is recorded in their own words:

> There came a man named Jesus and he chose us, when he was about thirty years old. Coming to Capernaum, he entered

[76] Tatian, influenced by his Encratite principles, changed John's diet to one of 'milk and honey' in his *Diatessaron*. See pp. 47, 117.

[77] Epiphanius, *Heresies* 30. 13.

[78] Cf. the tradition of the fire on Jordan at Jesus's baptism in Justin Martyr, *Dialogue with Trypho* 88. 3. See p. 144.

into the house of Simon, surnamed Peter, and he opened his mouth and said: 'As I was passing along by the lake of Tiberias I chose John and James, the sons of Zebedee, and Simon and Andrew, and Thaddaeus and Simon the Zealot and Judas Iscariot. As for you, Matthew, I called you when you were sitting at the tax office, and you followed me. I want you, therefore, to be my twelve apostles to bear witness to Israel.'[79]

Only eight apostles are listed; perhaps the others have dropped out in the transmission of the text. The list is basically Matthaean, but 'Simon the Zealot' (cf. Luke 6. 15; Acts 1. 13) replaces the synonymous 'Simon the Cananaean' of Matthew 10. 4 (cf. Mark 3. 18), as being more intelligible. The designation 'the lake of Tiberias' is unknown to the Synoptic Gospels; in the New Testament it is peculiar to John (6. 1; 21. 1). The statement that Jesus was 'about thirty years old' is derived from Luke 3. 23.

The Ebionites rejected the Old Testament sacrificial law as not authentic. Hence in their Gospel Jesus, who according to Matthew 5. 17 came not to abolish the law and the prophets but to fulfil them,[80] declares:

I came to abolish sacrifices, and if you do not cease from sacrificing, the wrath of God will not cease from you.[81]

Perhaps this was a sharpening of the words of Hosea 6. 6, 'I desire mercy, and not sacrifice', which Jesus quotes with approval in Matthew 9. 13 and 12. 7. Since the Passover involved a sacrifice, it met with the Ebionites' disapproval, the more so as it involved the eating of flesh, and so in their Gospel Jesus's answer to the disciples' question, 'Where will you have us prepare for you to eat the passover?' (Matthew 26. 17), is:

Do I desire with desire at this Passover to eat flesh with you?

[79] Epiphanius, *Heresies* 30. 13.
[80] See p. 61.
[81] Epiphanius, *Heresies* 30. 16.

This is readily recognised as the turning into a question (expecting a negative answer) of Jesus's statement to the disciples in Luke 22. 15: 'With desire I have desired to eat this passover with you before I suffer.'

Chapter Seven

The Gospel of Thomas

GREAT excitement was aroused at the end of last century and the beginning of the present one by the discovery of three Greek papyrus fragments at a place in Egypt which was known in Greek-speaking days as Oxyrhynchus.[1] The fragments, which were dated in the third century A.D., contained fifteen or sixteen isolated sayings ascribed to our Lord. They were introduced without any context apart from the introductory formula, 'Jesus said'. Some of them were quite similar to sayings ascribed to Jesus in our canonical Gospels; others were without any known parallel. One or two have passed into general currency, and have even been made the theme of latter-day hymns,[2] such as the saying: 'Wherever there are [two, they are not] without God, and where one is alone, [I say,] I am with him. Raise the stone, and there you will find me; cleave the wood, and there am I' (from P. Oxy. 1, discovered in 1897).[3]

One fragment (P. Oxy. 654, discovered in 1903) evidently preserved the preamble to a collection of such sayings; it contained the words: 'These are the life-giving words which were spoken by Jesus, who lives and appeared to Thomas and his ten companions. He said to them: "Whosoever hears these

[1] Oxyrhynchus was the name of a city of Egypt about 180 miles south of Alexandria (modern el-Benēsa). The papyri discovered there between 1896 and 1907 have been published in a series of 41 volumes (to date), the earlier volumes being edited by B. P. Grenfell and A. S. Hunt. The papyri are numbered serially according to the order of discovery and publication; each serial number is preceded by P. Oxy. (abbreviation for Oxyrhynchus Papyrus). P. Oxy. 1 was published (naturally) in Volume 1 (London, 1898), P. Oxy. 654 and 655 in Volume 4 (1904).

[2] Such as the hymn 'Those who love and those who labour', No. 669 in *Songs of Praise*, enlarged edition (Oxford, 1931), by 'G.D.' [Geoffrey Dearmer?].

[3] The words within square brackets fill in lacunae in the text. For the counterpart to this saying in the *Gospel of Thomas* see Sayings 30 (p. 126) and 77 (p. 142).

words shall never taste death."' Then follows the saying: 'Jesus said: "Let not him who seeks cease until he finds, and when he finds he will be astonished; astonished he will attain the kingdom, and having attained the kingdom he will rest."'

Some of these sayings were quoted independently by early Christian writers, and ascribed to various works which were in circulation in their day. But in quite recent years all these sayings, and nearly a hundred more, have been identified in a Coptic manuscript entitled (in its colophon or tailpiece) *The Gospel according to Thomas*, which begins with the preamble and saying about the kingdom quoted above.

This Coptic document is one of forty-nine, contained in thirteen leather-bound papyrus codices, which were discovered by a happy accident about 1945 near Nag Hammadi in Upper Egypt (some sixty miles north of Luxor).[4] These Coptic documents appear to have belonged to the library of a Gnostic community; most were translations from a Greek original.

The Coptic *Gospel of Thomas*, a fourth-century manuscript, is translated from a Greek text closely similar to, but not identical with, that to which the three Oxyrhynchus papyri (1, 654, 655) belonged. There is some internal evidence pointing to Syria as the place where the Greek collection originated; but in the course of its transmission in Egypt it may have taken on some Gnostic colouring. According to the Roman church father Hippolytus (early third century) a Gnostic group called the Naassenes used a *Gospel of Thomas*,[5] and this may well be the work to which he refers.

The Coptic version, first published in 1959,[6] is practically complete and contains the following 114 sayings (different editions vary a little in their numeration):

---

[4] Actually they appear to have been discovered in a large jar in a fourth-century Christian tomb at the foot of Jebel et-Tarif, about five miles north of Nag Hammadi and on the opposite (east) bank of the Nile. They were brought to Nag Hammadi and so are commonly known as the Nag Hammadi papyri. (While Nag Hammadi is some 60 miles north of Luxor when one travels round the bend of the Nile, it is only about 25 miles distant as the crow flies.)

[5] Hippolytus, *Refutation of Heresies* v. 7. 20.

[6] *The Gospel according to Thomas*, ed. A. Guillaumont, H.-Ch. Puech, G. Quispel, W. Till and Yassah 'Abd al Masih (Leiden and London, 1959). A useful English edition is provided in R. M. Grant and D. N. Freedman, *The Secret Sayings of Jesus* (Fontana Books, London, 1960).

Preamble

These are the secret words which Jesus the living one spoke and Didymus Judas Thomas wrote down.

'Jesus the living one' probably means 'Jesus the ever-living one'. It is common form in Gnostic Gospels to represent the esoteric teaching or *gnōsis* which they contain as delivered by Jesus to his chosen disciples during his appearances to them after he was raised from the dead.[7] But there is no esoteric flavour about the sayings collected in the *Gospel of Thomas*; many of them can be paralleled from the canonical Gospels (especially Luke) and many others are of the same matter-of-fact order. Perhaps it was not the sayings themselves but their interpretation in the circle from which the *Gospel of Thomas* came that the compiler regarded as 'secret'. As for the threefold name Didymus Judas Thomas, Didymus is the Greek word for 'twin' and is used in the Gospel of John (11. 16; 20. 24; 21.2) to explain Thomas, which is the Aramaic word for 'twin' (*t'ômâ*). In Syriac Christian tradition[8] he is identified with the 'Judas not Iscariot' who belonged to the company of the Twelve: in the Old Syriac Gospels the question of John 14. 22 is said to have been put to the Lord by 'Judas Thomas'.

Saying 1

And he said: 'Whosoever finds the interpretation of these words will never taste death.'

This confirms the impression made by the preamble, that the deeper interpretation of the sayings, not their surface meaning, pointed the way of salvation to initiates. The saying is quite similar to John 8. 51, where Jesus says, 'If any one keeps my word, he will never see death'—a statement which is taken up and repeated by his interlocutors in the form: 'If any one keeps my word, he will never *taste* death' (verse 52). But 'keep my word' means basically 'obey my commandment', not 'find its interpretation'—the intention in the Fourth Gospel is essentially

---

[7] E.g. in *Pistis Sophia* and *The Secret Doctrine of John*. Gnosticism presented the gospel in terms of salvation from the bondage of the material order by the reception and application of true knowledge (Greek *gnosis*).

[8] Especially in the *Acts of Thomas*, a third-century Gnostic romance in Syriac, in which he is the twin brother of Jesus.

ethical, whereas that in the *Gospel of Thomas* is mainly intellectual.

Saying 2

Jesus said: 'Let not him who seeks desist until he finds. When he finds he will be troubled; when he is troubled he will marvel, and he will reign over the universe.'

The Coptic wording deviates slightly from the Greek wording of P. Oxy, 654. 2, reproduced in translation above (p. 111). Clement of Alexandria quotes practically the same saying from the *Gospel according to the Hebrews*.[9]

Saying 3

Jesus said: '(*a*) If those who entice you say to you, "See, the kingdom is in heaven!" – then the birds of heaven will be there before you. If they say to you, "It is in the sea!" – then the fish will be there before you. But the kingdom is within you – and without as well. (*b*) If you know yourselves you will be known and you will know that you are the sons of the living Father. But if you do not know yourselves, then you are in destitution, and you yourselves are the destitution.'

This seems to be an expansion of the saying in Luke 17. 21: 'The kingdom of God is not coming with signs to be observed; nor will they say, "Lo, here it is!" or "There!" for behold, the kingdom of God is within you' (or 'in the midst of you').[10] But the *Gospel of Thomas* does not speak of the kingdom of *God*; it avoids the use of 'God' as the name of the heavenly Father (cf. comment on Saying 100).[11] The kingdom consists here in true knowledge of what is within and without. Francis Thompson's poem 'The Kingdom of God' (beginning 'O world invisible, we view thee') was based on the Greek text of these words from P. Oxy. 654. 3.

---

[9] Clement, *Miscellanies* ii. 45. 5; v. 96. 3. For the *Gospel according to the Hebrews* see pp. 99 ff.
[10] Cf. Saying 113 (p. 153).
[11] The kingdom may be called 'the kingdom of heaven' (Saying 20) or 'the kingdom of the Father' (Sayings 57, 113).

Saying 4
Jesus said: 'Let not the old man who is full of days hesitate to ask the child of seven days about the place of life; then he will live. For many that are first will be last, and they will become a single one.'

The point of this saying is at least superficially similar to that of canonical sayings about children, such as 'whoever does not receive the kingdom of God like a child shall not enter it' (Mark 10. 15). After the words 'many that are first will be last' the Greek text (P. Oxy. 654. 4) adds 'and the last, first' (cf. Mark 10. 31, etc.); this has probably been omitted by accident from our Coptic text. The 'single one' at the end of the saying is the personality that has finally transcended differentiation of age and sex – the latter is an ideal which finds recurring expression in the *Gospel of Thomas* (cf. Sayings 11, 16, 23, 49, 75, 106, 114). The underlying thought is that Adam, as first created, was androgynous, before being divided into male and female (Genesis 2. 21–23); the pristine arrangement will be restored in the life to come.[12]

Saying 5
Jesus said: 'Recognise what is before your face, and what is hidden will be revealed to you. For there is nothing hidden which will not be made manifest.'

The Greek text (P. Oxy. 654. 5) adds: 'or buried, which will not be revealed.' The closest canonical parallel is Luke 10. 2 (cf. Matthew 10. 26): 'Nothing is covered up that will not be revealed, or hidden that will not be known.' The same sentiment is expressed at the end of Saying 6.

Saying 6
His disciples questioned him; they said: 'Do you wish us to fast? How shall we pray and give alms, and what shall we feed upon?' Jesus said: 'Tell no falsehood and do not [to others] what is hateful to yourselves; for all these things are manifest in the sight of heaven. Nothing hidden will fail to

[12] This belief is ascribed to the Naassenes by Hippolytus, *Refutation* v. 6.5; 7.14 f. See Appendix to this chapter (p. 157).

be revealed and nothing concealed will fail to be blazed abroad.'

In this and other sayings (cf. Sayings 14, 27, 104) it is insisted that true fasting is abstinence from evil words and actions, not from indifferent things like food. The negative form of the golden rule, 'Do not [to others] what is hateful to yourselves', appears repeatedly in early Jewish ethics, e.g. Tobit 4. 15 ('What you hate, do not to any one') and Hillel's words in TB *Shabbath* 31a ('What is hateful to you, do not to your fellow; this is the whole law; everything else is commentary').

With the Greek text of this saying P. Oxy. 654 breaks off.

Saying 7
Jesus said: 'Happy is the lion whom the man eats, so that the lion becomes man; but woe to the man whom the lion eats, so that the man becomes lion!'

The point of this seems to be that a lion, if eaten by a man, is ennobled by rising in the scale of being, whereas a man, if eaten by a lion, is degraded to a lower status than was originally his and may even risk missing the goal of immortality. It is not that we become what we eat but that what we eat becomes part of us (as in Walter de la Mare's poem 'Little Miss T—'). Whether, in addition, there is any special symbolism in the lion, as in 1 Peter 5. 8 ('Your adversary the devil prowls around like a roaring lion, seeking some one to devour'), is exceedingly difficult to determine. (See also Saying 11.)

Saying 8
Then he said: 'Man is like a wise fisherman who casts his net into the sea. He brought it up out of the sea full of little fishes, in the midst of which this wise fisherman found a large, excellent fish. He threw all the little fishes back into the sea; without hesitation he chose the big fish. He who has ears to hear, let him hear!'

This, the first of many parables in the *Gospel of Thomas*, bears a superficial resemblance to the parable of the dragnet in Matthew 13. 47–50, but its point is closer to that of the parables of the treasure concealed in a field (Saying 109) and the pearl of great price (Saying 76), to gain which a man sells all that he has (Matthew 13. 44–46). In this context the big fish is either the true Gnostic, whom Christ chooses above all others, or the true knowledge for which the Gnostic abandons everything else.[13]

Saying 9

Jesus said: 'See, the sower went out, he filled his hand and scattered (the seeds). Some fell on the road; the birds came and picked them up. Some fell on the rock; they were quite unable to take root in the earth and sent forth no ears up to heaven. Some fell among thorns; they choked the seeds and the worm devoured them. But some fell on good ground, and it brought forth good fruit; it yielded sixtyfold and a hundred and twentyfold.'

This is another version of the parable of the sower (or the parable of the four soils), recorded in all three Synoptic Gospels (Mark 4. 3–8; Matthew 13. 3–8; Luke 8. 5–8). The worm that attacked the seed sown among thorns is peculiar to this version. The 'rock' instead of 'rocky ground' is distinctively Lukan; the statement that the seed sown there 'sent forth no ears up to heaven' has been recognised as a Naassene thought.[14] The statement that the first lot of seed fell 'on' (not 'by') the road probably reflects the sense of the Aramaic preposition used by Jesus in telling the parable (the preposition may be rendered 'on' or 'by' according to the context).

Saying 10

Jesus said: 'I have cast fire on the world, and see, I am watching over it until it sets it aflame!'

This is almost identical with Luke 12. 49: 'I came to cast fire upon the earth; and would that it were already kindled!' From the context in which the Lukan saying occurs, it seems to be a figurative reference to the division which Jesus's ministry causes instead of peace on earth (see Saying 16).[15]

---

[13] Compare the lost sheep in Saying 107 (p. 151).
[14] Hippolytus (*Refutation* v. 8. 29) reproduces the Naassene interpretation of the parable.
[15] For the 'fire' cf. also Saying 82 (p. 144).

Saying 11

Jesus said: '(*a*) This heaven will pass away and that which is above it will pass away, and the dead are not living and the living will not die. (*b*) Today you eat dead things and make them alive, but when you are in the light, what will you do? On the day when you were one, you became two; but when you have become two, what will you do?'

The first part of the saying reminds us of Matthew 24. 35 (cf. Matthew 5. 18; Luke 16. 17): 'Heaven and earth will pass away, but my words will not pass away' – but it is not a close parallel. As for eating dead things, this probably means that when the flesh of dead animals is eaten by human beings it becomes part of a living body (cf. Saying 7).[16] The eating of flesh was probably discouraged, as making it more difficult to attain the light of immortality; the views of a vegetarian Syrian sect called the Encratites may have influenced the tradition in this and some other regards.[17] The words about being one and becoming two refer to the dividing of man into male and female (cf. Saying 4). If sex was to be transcended in the life to come, it was felt best that it should play no part in the present life (this may be a further Encratite trait).

Saying 12

The disciples said to Jesus: 'We know that you are going to leave us: who will be chief over us?' Jesus said to them: 'In the place to which you go, betake yourselves to James the Just, on whose behalf heaven and earth alike were made.'

This saying originated in a Jewish-Christian setting where James the Just, Jesus's brother, was regarded as the natural leader of Jesus's disciples after Jesus's departure. James was actually leader of the Jerusalem church for fifteen to twenty years, until his death in A.D. 62; his memory was revered and enhanced by legendary embellishments.[18] Here a high estimate is placed on his person: in Jewish thought the world was created for the sake of the Torah,[19] although in one rabbinical

[16] A similar Naassene saying is quoted by Hippolytus, *Refutation* v. 8. 32.
[17] See p. 107.
[18] See pp. 36, 105.
[19] *Assumption of Moses* 1. 2; *Genesis Rabbah* 1. 25 (Midrash Rabbah, see p. 55, n. 4).

utterance 'every single person is obliged to say: "The world was created for my sake."'[20]

Saying 13

Jesus said to his disciples: 'Compare me and tell me whom I am like.' Simon Peter said to him: 'You are like a holy angel.' Matthew said to him: 'You are like a wise man and a philosopher.' Thomas said to him: 'Master, my face is quite unable to grasp whom you are like, that I might express it.' Jesus said: 'I am not your Master, for you have been drinking; you are intoxicated with the bubbling spring which belongs to me and which I have spread abroad.' Then he took him and drew him aside, and spoke three words to him. When Thomas came back to his companions, they asked him: 'What did Jesus say to you?' Thomas answered: 'If I tell you one of the words which he spoke to me, you will take stones and throw them at me; and a fire will come out of the stones and burn you up!'

This conversation begins like that at Caesarea Philippi, recorded in all three Synoptic Gospels, where Jesus asks his disciples 'Who do men say that I am?' and then: 'But who do you say that I am?' (Mark 8. 27–29). But the answers given here are quite different from what we find in the canonical tradition, which is consistent with the historical circumstances of Jesus's ministry. Here the answers are attempts to depict Jesus as the Gnostic Revealer. Those who have imbibed the *gnōsis* which he imparts (the 'bubbling spring' which he has spread abroad) are not his servants but his friends,[21] and therefore 'Master' is an unsuitable title for them to give him. As for the three words spoken secretly to Thomas, conveying Jesus's hidden identity, they are probably the three secret words on which, according to the Naassenes, the existence of the world depended: *Kaulakau, Saulasau, Zeesar.*[22] (In fact, these three words are corruptions of the Hebrew phrases in Isaiah 28. 10, 13, translated 'Line upon line, precept upon precept, there a

[20] TB *Sanhedrin* 37b.
[21] Cf. John 15. 14.
[22] Hippolytus, *Refutation* v. 8. 4. Kaulakau, they said, was Adamas, primal man, 'the being who is on high' (cf. p. 139 with n. 45); Saulasau, mortal man here below; Zeesar, the Jordan which flows upward.

little' — but their origin was probably forgotten.) The followers of the Gnostic Basilides are said to have taught that Jesus descended 'in the name of *Kaulakau*'.[23] The fire that would come out of the stones is perhaps the fire of Saying 10. There is in any case ample attestation of the belief that the untimely divulging of a holy mystery can be as destructive as fire.

Saying 14
Jesus said to them: 'When you fast, you will bring sin upon yourselves; when you pray, you will be condemned; when you give alms, you will injure your spirit. When you enter any land and go through the countryside, when you are entertained, eat what is set before you and heal the sick in those places. For nothing that enters into your mouth will defile you, but it is what comes out of your mouth that will defile you.'

Fasting, prayer and almsgiving (cf. Saying 6) are three forms of piety mentioned in the Sermon on the Mount (Matthew 6. 1–18), but the instructions given here are quite different from those given there. Such pious activities, it appears, are superfluous and indeed harmful for the true Gnostic. (Similar sentiments about prayer and fasting are expressed in Saying 104.) The second and third sentences in the saying are respectively parallel to Luke 10. 8 f. and Matthew 15. 11 (cf. Mark 7. 15). The addition to the injunction 'eat what is set before you' of the words denying that food conveys defilement underlines the relevance of the injunction to the Gentile mission (cf. Acts 10. 15; 1 Corinthians 10. 27).

Saying 15
Jesus said: 'When you see him who was not born of woman, prostrate yourselves with your face to the ground and adore him: he is your Father.'

But for the last clause, we might have interpreted this saying to mean that Jesus — unlike John the Baptist (cf. Saying 46) — was not born of woman. But whatever the compiler or editor believed about the mode of Jesus's coming into the world (see

[23] Irenaeus, *Heresies* i. 24. 6.

Saying 19a), this is probably not in view here, since Jesus and the Father are distinguished (cf. Saying 3). Even so, he would no doubt have drawn his own conclusions from such a saying of Jesus as that of John 10. 30: 'I and the Father are one.' The Father is in any case the unbegotten One.

Saying 16
Jesus said: 'Verily, people think that I have come to send peace on the world. But they do not realise that I have come to send on earth dissensions, fire, sword and war. Verily, if there are five in a house, they will find themselves ranged three against two and two against three—father against son and son against father—and they will stand singly.'

This saying is for the most part a reproduction of Luke 12. 51–53 (cf. Matthew 10. 34–36); the statement that 'they will stand singly' suggests that the true Gnostic gets along better without family ties. (Cf. Saying 55.)

Saying 17
Jesus said: 'I will give you what eye never saw, what ear never heard, what hand never touched, and what never entered the heart of man.'

This saying has no parallel in the canonical Gospels, but it is very similar to the quotation in 1 Corinthians 2. 9 which Paul introduces by 'as it is written'—a clause which normally indicates an Old Testament source. Here, however, we have no Old Testament quotation (the resemblance to Isaiah 64. 4 is superficial); according to Origen and others it is a quotation from the *Secrets* (or *Apocalypse*) *of Elijah*.[24] Like the *Gospel of Thomas*, the second-century work called the *Acts of Peter* ascribes the saying to Jesus.[25] In its present context it perhaps belongs to a Naassene formula of initiation. Whereas Paul quotes the words with reference to the hidden wisdom which his Corinthian converts are unable to grasp because of their

[24] Origen, *Commentary on Matthew* 27. 9; Jerome, *Commentary on Isaiah* 64. 4; Ambrosiaster, *Commentary on 1 Corinthians* 2. 9.
[25] *Acts of Peter* 39.

spiritual immaturity and lack of brotherly love, here they are probably intended to recommend that kind of 'knowledge' on which the Corinthians, in Paul's judgment, concentrated too much. It has also been suggested that they were used by Gnostics as a counterblast to the anti-Gnostic claim in 1 John 1. 1 to bear witness only to that 'which we have heard, which we have seen with our eyes, which we have looked upon and touched with our hands'.[26] (The clause 'what hand never touched', unparalleled in 1 Corinthians 2. 9, may echo 1 John 1. 1.)

Saying 18

The disciples said to Jesus: 'Tell us what our end will be like.' Jesus said: 'Have you then unveiled the beginning, that you should ask about the end? For where the beginning is, there the end will be. Happy is he who stands at the beginning: he will know the end and will not taste death.'

This saying is reminiscent of 2 Esdras 7. 30 ('the world shall be as it was at the first beginnings'), but perhaps it is to be understood in the sense of Revelation 22. 13, where Jesus says: 'I am the Alpha and the Omega, the first and the last, the beginning and the end.' (For 'not tasting death' we may compare Saying 1.)

Saying 19

Jesus said: '(a) Happy is he who existed before he was born. (b) If you become my disciples and hear my words, these stones will minister to you. For you have five trees in Paradise which are unmoved in summer or winter, and their leaves do not fall. Whoever knows them will not taste death.'

The one who existed before he was born is Jesus himself, who 'came from the Father and entered into the world' (John 16. 28). Saying 19a is quoted by other early Christian writers: Irenaeus and Lactantius quote it as a prophetic utterance of Jeremiah.[27]

---

[26] Cf. A. A. T. Ehrhardt, *The Framework of the New Testament Stories* (Manchester U.P., 1964), pp. 29 ff.

[27] Irenaeus, *Demonstration of the Apostolic Preaching* 43; Lactantius, *Divine Institutions* iv. 8. The words may have occurred in an apocryphal work, no longer extant, ascribed to Jeremiah.

The reference to the stones in Saying 19b is reminiscent of the turning of stones into bread in the temptation narrative (Matthew 4. 3; Luke 4. 3). The five trees have the property of the unfailing 'tree of life' in Revelation 22. 2; they are five in number perhaps because they are envisaged as spiritual counterparts to the five natural senses.[28]

Saying 20
The disciples said to Jesus: 'Tell us what the kingdom of heaven is like.' He said to them: 'It is like a mustard seed, smaller than all seeds. But when it falls on the cultivated ground, it puts forth a large branch and provides shelter for (the) birds of heaven.'[29]

This is quite close to the parable of the mustard seed in the three Synoptic Gospels (Mark 4. 30–32; Matthew 13. 31 f.; Luke 13. 18 f.), except that there Jesus does not tell the parable in response to the disciples' question, but introduces it with a rhetorical question of his own.

Saying 21
(a) Mary[30] said to Jesus: 'Whom do your disciples resemble?' He said to her: 'They are like children who have gone into a field which does not belong to them. When the owners of the field come, they [the children] will say, "Leave us our field!" And the owners divest themselves in their presence so as to leave them their field, and hand it over to them. (b) Therefore I say to you, If the owner of the house knows that the thief is coming, he will keep awake and not allow him to break into his royal dwelling so as to carry off his goods. So you must be on your guard in face of the world. Gird your loins with great strength, so that the bandits may find no way to get at you and seize the advantage against which you are prepared. (c) If there is a man of understanding among you,

---

[28] The Gnostic treatise *Pistis Sophia* makes repeated mention of the 'five trees' in the 'treasury of the light'.
[29] The Naassene interpretation of the parable of the mustard seed is summarised in Hippolytus, *Refutation* v. 9. 6: the mustard seed in this interpretation is 'the indivisible point existing in the body which only he who is spiritual knows'.
[30] Presumably Mary Magdalene; see Saying 114 (p. 153).

then, when the fruit has come, he has gone in haste, sickle in hand, and reaped it. He who has ears to hear, let him hear!'

Here we have three essentially independent sayings loosely linked together by a superficial community of vocabulary or theme. The call for vigilance in Saying 21b (cf. Saying 103) is an amplification of the saying found in Matthew 24. 43 and Luke 12. 39; the house to be guarded is now a royal palace, and the crisis for which the disciples must be prepared is not the coming of the Son of Man but the constant encroachment of the material world. The 'bandits' are trying to invade the divine or heavenly element in man. For the injunction to the disciples to gird their loins cf. Luke 12. 35. Saying 21c is an adaptation of the parable of the seed growing secretly in Mark 4. 26–29. Saying 21a has no canonical parallel: perhaps the point is that, as the owner of the house in Saying 21b refuses to admit the bandits, so the children in the field refuse to give it up to others who claim it. But the point is obscure, and there could be a connection with the next saying, which also refers to children.

Saying 22

Jesus saw some infants at the breast. He said to his disciples: 'These children at the breast are like those who enter the kingdom.' They said to him: 'Shall we, then, enter the kingdom as children?' Jesus said to them: 'When you make the two one, and when you make the inner as the outer and the outer as the inner and the above as the below, and when you make the male and the female one, so that the male is no longer male and the female no longer female, when you make eyes in place of an eye, and a hand in place of a hand, and a foot in place of a foot, an image in place of an image, then you will enter the kingdom.'

This is an expansion of the canonical saying: 'whoever does not receive the kingdom of God like a child shall not enter it' (Luke 18. 17; cf. Matthew 18. 3). But the expansion suggests the abolition of sex distinction (cf. Sayings 4, 11, 106): as infants are devoid of sex awareness or shame, so should the disciples be. In the *Gospel according to the Egyptians* words like these are spoken by Jesus to Salome.[31] We may recognise a Gnostic interpretation of Paul's words: 'there can be no male and female' (Galatians 3. 28). The replacement of physical eyes, hand and foot by corresponding spiritual members is probably a gloss on the saying in Mark 9. 43–48 (cf. Matthew 5. 29 f.; 18. 8 f.), which similarly follows words about children.

Saying 23
Jesus said: 'I will choose you, one among a thousand and two among ten thousand, and they will stand as a single one.'

However many are called, only a few are chosen (for one in a thousand cf. Ecclesiastes 7. 28).[32] The last clause is practically identical with that of Saying 16 (cf. also Sayings 74, 75).

Saying 24
His disciples said to him: 'Show us the place where you are, for we must seek it.' He said to them: 'He who has ears, let him hear! There is light within a man of light, and it illuminates the whole world; if it does not illuminate it, it is darkness.'

The disciples' question is like that of John 13. 36 ff., transposed into the present tense; the answer about light and darkness is based on such canonical sayings as Matthew 6. 22 f.; Mark 4. 21 and Luke 11. 33–36. But the 'light' here is the true knowledge: the 'man of light' is the enlightened Gnostic. (Cf. Sayings 50, 77.)

Saying 25
Jesus said: 'Love your brother as your own soul; guard him like the apple of your eye.'

This is in line with canonical sayings of Jesus which enjoin brotherly love on his disciples;[33] in the *Gospel of Thomas* the 'brother' is perhaps the fellow-Gnostic.

[31] See Appendix to this chapter (p. 157).
[32] It is a presupposition of Gnostic thought in general that the saved form a very small élite.
[33] Cf. Saying 5b quoted above (p. 102) from the *Gospel according to the Hebrews*.

Saying 26
Jesus said: 'You see the splinter which is in your brother's eye, but you do not see the plank which is in your own eye. When you have removed the plank from your own eye, then you will see to remove the splinter from your brother's eye.'

This is parallel to a saying in the Sermon on the Mount (Matthew 7. 3–5; Luke 6. 41 f.). P. Oxy. 1 begins with the Greek text of this saying.

Saying 27
[Jesus said:] 'If you do not fast in relation to the world, you will not find the kingdom. If you do not keep the true sabbath, you will not see the Father.'

This saying (whose Greek text is preserved in P. Oxy. 1. 2) seems to have been widely known in the church of the second and third centuries; its substance appears in Justin, Clement of Alexandria and Tertullian.[34] While literal fasting and sabbath-keeping are deprecated (cf. Sayings 14, 104), the spiritual counterpart to these religious exercises is recommended (cf. Saying 6).

Saying 28
Jesus said: 'I stood in the midst of the world and I manifested myself in the flesh to these. I found them all intoxicated; I found none thirsty among them. And my soul was grieved for the children of men, because they are blind in heart and do not see; because they have come into the world empty, they still seek to go out of the world empty. But may some-one come and set them right! Then, when they have slept themselves sober, they will repent.'

The Greek original of this saying appears in P. Oxy. 1. 3. While a genuine concern for the blindness and ignorance of men is here expressed, it is the concern of one who has come to impart secret knowledge rather than of one who has come to

[34] Justin, *Dialogue with Trypho* 12. 3; Clement, *Miscellanies* iii. 99. 4; Tertullian, *Against the Jews* 4.

lay down his life for them; the latter idea is absent from the *Gospel of Thomas*.[35]

Saying 29

Jesus said: 'If the flesh was brought into being for the sake of the spirit, it is a miracle; but if the spirit [was brought into being] for the sake of the flesh, it is a miracle of miracles. I marvel how this great wealth has taken up residence in this poverty.'

Flesh and spirit are antithetical: spirit does not need flesh as its vehicle, and it is unthinkable that spirit exists to aid flesh. In the conditions of earthly life, spirit is the 'great wealth' that resides in the 'poverty' of a mortal body (cf. Sayings 85, 87, 112).

Saying 30

Jesus said: 'Where there are three gods, there are gods. Where there are two, or [even] one, I am with him.'

The Greek text of P. Oxy. 1. 4 is more intelligible: 'Where there are [two, they are not] without God, and where there is one alone, [I say,] I am with him. Raise the stone, and there you will find me; cleave the wood, and there am I.' (For the last sentence see Saying 77.) The Coptic version may be based on a defective copy of the Greek text; it is conceivable, but not very likely, that it dismisses as tritheism attempts to state the orthodox doctrine of the Trinity. In general we can recognise an amplification of the canonical saying: 'Where two or three are gathered together in my name, there am I in the midst of them' (Matthew 18. 20).

Saying 31

Jesus said: 'A prophet is not welcomed in his own town, and a physician works no cure on those who know him.'

---

[35] Cf. the words of the prophet of God (Hermes) in the *Corpus Hermeticum* 1. 27: 'I have begun to proclaim to men the beauty of piety and knowledge: "O ye peoples, earth-born men who have given yourselves over to drunkenness and sleep and ignorance of God, sober up and cease to be intoxicated and bewitched by irrational sleep"' (similar language is used in 7. 1).

The saying about the prophet is found in the Synoptic and Johannine traditions alike (Mark 6. 4; John 4. 44). The saying about the physician resembles 'Physician, heal yourself', a proverb quoted in Luke 4. 23 immediately before the Lukan occurrence of the saying about the prophet; Luke 4. 23 f. may therefore be the source of this composite formulation.

Saying 32
Jesus said: 'A city built on a high mountain, and well-fortified, cannot fall, neither can it be hidden.'

This saying amplifies that of Matthew 5. 14b by emphasising the impregnability as well as the conspicuousness of the 'city set on a hill'.

Saying 33
Jesus said: 'What you hear with your ear, proclaim in another ear on your house-tops. For no one lights a lamp and puts it under a bushel or puts it in a hidden place; but one puts it on the lampstand, so that all who go in and out may see its light.'

This is a combination of two sayings, both of which enjoin public testimony. The first is parallel to Matthew 10. 27b ('what you hear whispered, proclaim upon the house-tops'), which is preceded by a reference to light (verse 27a); this reference provides the transition to the second saying, which is similar to Luke 8. 16 and 11. 33 (cf. Mark 4. 21; Matthew 5. 15).

Saying 34
Jesus said: 'If a blind man leads another blind man, both fall into the ditch.'

This proverb appears in the canonical tradition in Matthew 15. 14b and Luke 6. 39.

Saying 35
Jesus said: 'It is not possible for anyone to enter the strong man's house and take it by force unless he binds his hands; then he will ransack his house.'

This is practically identical with the canonical saying of Mark 3. 27 and parallels (Matthew 12. 29; Luke 11. 21 f.). In the Synoptic Gospels the 'strong man' is Beelzebul, prince of the demonic realm; here he may be rather the guardian of the material order.

Saying 36
Jesus said: 'Have no anxiety, from morning to evening and from evening to morning, about what you will put on again.'

A variant form of this saying appears in Greek in P. Oxy. 655. 1. The saying is to much the same effect as Matthew 6. 25 and Luke 12. 22 ('do not be anxious about your ... body, what you shall put on'); but in the *Gospel of Thomas* it is perhaps interpreted in the same sense as the saying which follows.

Saying 37
His disciples said to him: 'When will you appear to us? When shall we see you?' Jesus said: 'When you disrobe yourselves without being ashamed, when you take off your garments and lay them at your feet as small children do, and trample on them, then you will become the sons of the Living One, and you will have no fear.'

The Greek original of the first part of this saying is preserved in P. Oxy. 655. 2. The disciples' question is reminiscent of the questions of Matthew 24. 3 (cf. Mark 13. 4; Luke 21. 7) and Luke 17. 20; but the answer is quite different from anything found in the canonical Gospels. As the primal sin in Eden was followed by a sense of shame at the awareness of being naked, so (it is implied) the restoration of primal innocence will be marked by the removal of such a sense of shame.[36] For the reference to small children cf. Saying 22; for 'sons of the Living One' cf. Saying 3.

Saying 38
Jesus said: 'You have often desired to hear these words which I speak to you, but you have no one else from whom to

[36] For trampling on the garments cf. the *Gospel according to the Egyptians*; see Appendix to this chapter (p. 157).

hear them. The days will come when you will seek me but will not find me.'

The closest canonical counterpart to this saying is Luke 17. 22, but whereas that refers to the future advent of the Son of Man, this refers to the present teaching of Jesus. A modicum of futurity survives, however, after the pattern of John 7. 34: 'you will seek me and you will not find me'.

Saying 39
Jesus said: 'The Pharisees and the scribes have taken the keys of knowledge and hidden them; they have neither entered in themselves nor allowed those who wished to enter in to do so. But as for you, be prudent as serpents and harmless as doves.'

This saying (the Greek original of which is preserved fragmentarily in P. Oxy. 655. 3) is practically identical in its first part with Luke 11. 52 and in its second part with Matthew 10. 16b. The 'knowledge' (*gnōsis*) of the first part was probably interpreted in a Gnostic sense; the same idea is expressed in Saying 102. As for the second part, the Naassenes or Ophites (from the Hebrew and Greek words for 'serpent', *nahash* and *ophis* respectively) may have seen special significance in the 'prudence' of the serpent.

Saying 40
Jesus said: 'A vine was planted outside of the Father. It did not gain strength; it will be pulled up by the root and will perish.'

Cf. Matthew 15. 13: 'Every plant which my heavenly Father has not planted will be rooted up.' There is a remoter parallel in John 15. 6, in the parable of the true vine.

Saying 41
Jesus said: 'He who has in hand, to him will be given; but he who has not, [even] the little that he has will be taken from him.'

This is practically identical with Matthew 25. 29 and Luke 19. 26.

Saying 42
Jesus said: 'Be like those who pass over.'

In other words, do not settle down here. These words are later ascribed to Jesus in some strands of Muslim tradition (although in other strands they are ascribed to Muhammad or to one of his companions). The most famous instance of their ascription to Jesus in Muslim tradition is on the main gateway of the mosque erected in 1601 at Fathpur-Sikri, south of Delhi, by the Moghul Akbar the Great; it bears the inscription: 'Jesus, on whom be peace, said: "This world is a bridge. Pass over it; but do not build your dwelling there."'[37]

Saying 43
His disciples said to him: 'Who are you who tell us these things?' [He said:] 'Do you not recognise who I am by the things I say to you? But you yourselves have become like the Jews; they love the tree and hate its fruit; they love the fruit and hate the tree.'

This disciples' question is like that of the Jews to Jesus in John 8. 25; Jesus's answer, with its implied insistence that tree and fruit are of the same kind (cf. Saying 45), may be derived from the saying in Matthew 7. 16–20 and Luke 6. 43 f. The anti-Jewish sentiment recognisable in several places throughout the *Gospel of Thomas* becomes quite explicit here.

Saying 44
Jesus said: 'He who has blasphemed the Father will be forgiven, and he who has blasphemed the Son will be forgiven; but he who has blasphemed the Holy Spirit will not be forgiven, neither on earth nor in heaven.'

---

[37] There is a full discussion of the history of this saying by J. Jeremias in *Unknown Sayings of Jesus* (S.P.C.K., London, 1964), pp. 111 ff. 'Here', he says, 'is a noble expression of the thought which the author of Hebrews puts into other words: "Here we have no lasting city, but we seek the city which is to come" (13. 14).'

This is a development of the saying found in Luke 12. 10 (cf. also Mark 3. 28 f.; Matthew 12. 32). Whereas the canonical saying contrasts the unpardonable sin of blasphemy against the Holy Spirit with the relatively venial sin of blasphemy against the Son of Man, the *Gospel of Thomas* (surprisingly) adds blasphemy against the Father as relatively venial. The formulation is trinitarian, as that in the canonical Gospels is not. For the phrase 'neither on earth nor in heaven', cf. Matthew 12. 32: 'neither in this age nor in the age to come'. The *Gospel of Thomas* prefers a form of words which is not eschatological.

Saying 45
Jesus said: 'People do not gather grapes from briars, nor do they pick figs from camel's thorn. These give no fruit. A good man brings forth what is good from his store, but a bad man brings forth what is bad from *his* store, which is in his heart, and he speaks bad things; for out of the abundance of his heart he speaks bad things.'

The natural correspondence between tree and fruit, glanced at in Saying 43, is here elaborated in a saying closely resembling Luke 6. 43–46 (cf. Matthew 7. 16–20; James 3. 12a).

Saying 46
Jesus said: 'From Adam to John the Baptist, among those born of women none is greater than John the Baptist. But lest your eyes [should be blinded] I have said: "He who is least among you will come to know the kingdom, and will be more exalted than John."'

This saying echoes the well-known words of Jesus in Matthew 11. 11 and Luke 7. 28; but here the meaning probably is that the true Gnostic is more exalted than even the greatest of men excluded from the privileged circle.

Saying 47
Jesus said: 'No one can ride two horses or draw two bows at once. And no servant can serve two masters, otherwise he will honour the one and be roughly treated by the other. No one ever drinks old wine and desires the same instant to drink

new wine; new wine is not poured into old skins, lest they burst, nor is old wine poured into new skins, lest it spoils. And no one sews an old patch on to a new garment, for a rent would be made.'

The canonical saying about the impossibility of serving two masters (Matthew 6. 24; Luke 16. 13) is here amplified by two illustrations from life, and followed by sayings contrasting the old order and the new, sufficiently similar to Luke 5. 36–39 (cf. Mark 2. 21 f.; Matthew 9. 16 f.), but with secondary deviations. The canonical counterparts do not speak of pouring old wine into new skins, or of patching a new garment with an old piece of cloth. These deviations are probably deliberate: the true Gnostic will not allow his new doctrine to be encumbered with relics from the past.

Saying 48
Jesus said: 'If two are together in peace in the same house, they will say to the mountain, "Move over!" – and it will move over.'

This is reminiscent of the promise of an affirmative answer to the prayer of any two who 'agree on earth about anything they ask' (Matthew 18. 19). A similar promise in Mark 11. 24, which does not specify 'two', is preceded by the words: 'whoever says to this mountain, "Be taken up and cast into the sea", and does not doubt in his heart, but believes that what he says will come to pass, it will be done for him' (Mark 11. 23). The *Gospel of Thomas* either conflates the two passages, or depends on an earlier compilation or Gospel harmony which conflated them. (Cf. Saying 106 for the underlying significance.)

Saying 49
Jesus said: 'Happy are the single and the chosen ones, for you will find the kingdom. Because you have come forth from it, you will return there again.'

For the 'single' ones see Sayings 4 and 23; in the latter, being 'single' and being 'chosen' are associated as here. In Gnostic

belief the spiritual element in man comes from the upper realm
of light and is destined to return there.

Saying 50

Jesus said: 'If people ask you, "Where have you come from?"
say to them, "We have come from the light, from the place
where light is self-originated. It [stood] and manifested itself
in their image." If they say to you, "Who are you?" say, "We
are his sons, we are the chosen ones of the living Father."
If they ask you, "What is the sign of your Father within
you?" say to them, "It is a movement and a rest."'

The subject-matter of this saying is much the same as that
of Saying 49; for the place of light cf. Sayings 24, 77. The
relationship to the living Father has been mentioned in
Saying 3 (cf. Saying 37). For the 'image' see Saying 83. The
'movement' may be the re-ascent to the realm of light; the 'rest'
is probably that which is the goal of the true Gnostic (Sayings 1
[Greek], 51, 90).[38]

Saying 51

His disciples said to him: 'On what day will the rest of the
dead take place, and on what day will the new world come?'
He said to them: 'This rest for which you wait has come
already, and you have not recognised it!'

The theme of 'rest' is carried on from Saying 50. But the
expectation of rest after death is here transformed into an
assurance that the Gnostic has attained true rest already. This
kind of transformation, not unlike that which Paul describes
ironically in 1 Corinthians 4. 8, is sometimes referred to as an
'over-realised eschatology' (cf. 2 Timothy 2. 18).

Saying 52

His disciples said to him: 'Twenty-four prophets spoke in
Israel and all of them spoke in you.' He said to them: 'You

---

[38] There may be a reference to the 'unmoved mover': according to Hippolytus (*Refutation* v. 7. 25), the Naassenes 'say that the being which moves
everything does not move, for while it produces everything it remains what
it is, without becoming any of the things that come into being'.

have forsaken the one who is alive before your eyes, and you have spoken of those who are dead.'

The number of the prophets corresponds to the number of books in the Hebrew Bible.[39] Throughout the New Testament it is emphasised that Christ has fulfilled the Old Testament scriptures: 'To him all the prophets bear witness' (Acts 10. 43).[40] But this saying reflects a disparaging attitude to the Old Testament common to several of the Gnostic schools. Augustine knew the saying, and dismissed it as an invention.[41]

Saying 53

His disciples said to him: 'Is circumcision profitable or not?' He said to them: 'If it were profitable, men's mothers would have borne them to their fathers already circumcised. But it is the true circumcision in the spirit that is profitable.'

Literal circumcision is rejected, like literal fasting and other religious exercises (cf. Saying 6). What counts is the spiritual counterparts of these, the elements of true heart-religion. That spiritual circumcision was the important thing was emphasised even in Old Testament times (cf. Deuteronomy 10. 16; Jeremiah 4. 4); Paul speaks to the same effect in Romans 2. 29; Philippians 3. 3; Colossians 2. 11.

Saying 54

Jesus said: 'Happy are the poor, for yours is the kingdom of heaven.'

This beatitude approximates to the form in Luke 6. 20, since it has simply 'the poor' as against 'the poor in spirit' of Matthew

[39] Another, but less probable, view is that the twenty-four prophets are the twenty-three listed in the old Jewish *Lives of the Prophets*, edited by C. C. Torrey (Philadelphia, 1943), with the addition of John the Baptist (Grant and Freedman, *The Secret Sayings of Jesus*, p. 153).

[40] Some translators and commentators treat 'in you' as though it meant 'concerning you'; it includes this, but goes beyond it. Christ, as the Logos, is the one in whom they prophesied — which is the reverse way of putting the New Testament statement that 'the Spirit of the Christ within them prophesied' (1 Peter 1. 11). Cf. A. A. T. Ehrhardt, 'The Disciples of Emmaus', *New Testament Studies* 10 (1963–64), p. 192; he compares the apocryphal *Epistle of the Apostles* 19 ('all the words which were spoken by the prophets were fulfilled in me, for I myself was in them').

[41] *Against an Adversary of the Law and the Prophets* 2. 14.

5. 3; but (as regularly in the *Gospel of Thomas*) it prefers the Matthaean 'kingdom of heaven' to 'kingdom of God' (see Sayings 3, 20).

Saying 55

Jesus said: 'He who does not hate his father and mother cannot be my disciple, and he who does not hate his brother and sister and take up his cross like me will not become worthy of me.'

This saying (cf. Saying 101) conflates Luke 14. 26 f. with Matthew 10. 37 f. The Lukan 'cannot be my disciple' and the Matthaean 'is not worthy of me' may go back to one and the same Aramaic original.[42] The interpretation of the words in the *Gospel of Thomas* may be that a Gnostic renounces family ties (cf. Saying 16). Unlike the disciple in Luke 14. 26, the true Gnostic probably has no wife and children to 'hate'.

Saying 56

Jesus said: 'He who has come to know the world has found a corpse, and as for him who has found a corpse, the world is not worthy of him.'

To say that the world is not worthy of someone (cf. Hebrews 11. 38) is to commend him; therefore (strange as it may seem) to find a corpse is praiseworthy. The Naassenes, according to Hippolytus, spoke of the spiritual body as a 'corpse'.[43] But the analogy of Saying 111 ('as for him who finds himself, the world is not worthy of him') suggests that here 'corpse' means 'body' as used in the sense of 'self'. If so, we may have a cryptic parallel to the canonical saying about gaining the world and losing one's own self, or *vice versa* (Luke 9. 24 f.; Matthew 16. 25 f.), which follows a saying about denying self and taking up the cross (cf. Saying 55).

Saying 57

Jesus said: 'The kingdom of the Father is like a man who

---

[42] Cf. T. W. Manson, *The Teaching of Jesus* (C.U.P., 1935), pp. 237 ff.
[43] The reason for this strange use of 'corpse' was that the spiritual essence is 'buried' in the body as a corpse is buried in a tomb (Hippolytus, *Refutation* v. 8. 22).

had [good] seed [in his field]. By night his enemy came and sowed tares over the good seed. This man did not allow the tares to be pulled up, "for fear", he said to them [his servants], "that when you go to pull up the tares you pull up the wheat with them. In truth, by harvest-time the tares will have become recognisable; they can be pulled up and burned".'

This is substantially the same as the parable of the tares (darnel) in Matthew 13. 24–30.

Saying 58
Jesus said: 'Happy is the man who has laboured: he has found life.'

This is remotely similar to Matthew 11. 28 f., where those who labour are promised that they will find rest (cf. Saying 90 for a closer parallel).

Saying 59
Jesus said: 'Look towards the Living One as long as you are alive, lest when you die you seek to see him and cannot.'

There is a general resemblance between this saying and John 7. 34: 'you will seek me and you will not find me; where I am you cannot come' (cf. John 13. 33).

Saying 60
[They saw] a Samaritan carrying a lamb on his way into Judaea. He said to his disciples: 'What is this man doing with the lamb?' They said to him: 'He is going to kill and eat it.' He said to them: 'As long as it is alive he will not eat it, but only if he kills it and it becomes a corpse.' They said to him: 'In no other way can he do it.' He said to them: 'As for you, seek out a place of rest for yourselves, lest you become corpses and be eaten.'

This saying is superficially linked to Saying 59 by the recurrence of the clause, 'as long as it is (you are) alive'. But the incident of the Samaritan and the lamb is unparalleled, and its significance is obscure. The reference in Saying 11 to eating

dead things comes to mind, as also does the 'corpse' theme in
Saying 56. But attempts to allegorise the lamb differ widely.

Saying 61

Jesus said: 'Two will be resting there on one divan: one will
die, the other will live.' Salome said: 'Who are you, sir, and
whose son are you, that you have taken your place on my
divan and eaten from my table?' Jesus said to her: 'I am he
who derives his being from him who is the Same; to me has
been given from what belongs to my Father.' 'I am your
disciple' [said she]. 'Therefore [said he], I tell you this:
when one is united, he will be full of light; when he is divided,
he will be full of darkness.'

The first part of the saying is similar to what is said about the
day of crisis in Luke 17. 34. Salome is more prominent in the
apocryphal writings than in the canonical Gospels, where a
comparison of Mark 15. 40 with Matthew 27. 56 suggests that
she was the wife of Zebedee and the mother of James and
John.[44] The translation of Jesus's conversation with her is
uncertain, but the main point seems to be that the perfect state
involves a return to the pristine unity of male and female (cf.
Saying 4). 'He who is the Same' (others render 'who is my
equal') is synonymous with the Father of Jesus, who is un-
changing perhaps in the sense of being undifferentiated.

Saying 62

Jesus said: 'I tell my mysteries to those [who are worthy of]
my mysteries. Let not your left hand know what your right
hand does.'

The first sentence is similar to the canonical saying about the
disciples receiving the mystery of the kingdom of God which
remains a riddle to outsiders (Mark 4. 11 f.; cf. Matthew 13.
11 ff.; Luke 8. 10); but here the esoteric doctrine of the
Gnostics is meant. The second sentence in the canonical
tradition (Matthew 6. 3) enjoins secrecy in generous giving;

[44] See pp. 86, 165. In the *Gospel according to the Egyptians* she is childless
(see p. 157).

here it forbids the spreading of the esoteric doctrine beyond the privileged circle.

Saying 63

Jesus said: 'There was a rich man who had much money. He said: "I will use my money to sow and reap and plant and fill my storehouses with fruit, so that I may lack nothing." So he thought in his heart. But during that night he died. He who has ears to hear, let him hear!'

This is an abbreviated form of the parable of the rich fool (Luke 12. 16–21). See also Saying 88.

Saying 64

Jesus said: 'A certain man had invited guests. When he had prepared the feast, he sent his servant to summon those guests. He went to the first and said to him: "My master calls you!" He replied: "I have money to receive from merchants; they are coming to me tonight and I must go and give them orders. I beg to be excused from the feast." The servant went to another guest and said: "My master calls you!" He said to him: "I have bought a house and must devote a day's work to it. I shall have no time." He went to another and said to him: "My master calls you!" He answered him: "My friend is going to get married, and I have to arrange his wedding feast. I shall not be able to go; I beg to be excused from the feast." He went to another and said to him: "My master calls you!" He said to him: "I have bought a farm and I have not yet gone to collect the rent of it; I beg to be excused from the feast." The servant went back and told his master: "Those whom you invited to the feast have begged to be excused." The master said to his servant: "Go out into the streets and bring in whomsoever you find, so that they may dine." Tradesmen and merchants shall not enter my Father's places.'

This is a version of the parable of the great supper in Luke 14. 16–24, although the details of the excuses differ (cf. Matthew 22. 5: 'But they made light of it and went off, one to his farm, another to his business'). The last sentence seems to be regarded as Jesus's own comment, and brings the tradesmen and merchants out of the parable into the moral (cf. Zechariah 14. 21b: 'there shall no longer be a trader in the house of the LORD of hosts on that day').

Saying 65
He said: 'A good man had a vineyard which he let out to cultivators so that they might work in it and he might receive the fruit from them. He sent his servant so that the cultivators might give him the fruit of the vineyard. They seized his servant, beat him and nearly killed him. The servant came and told his master. His master said: "Perhaps he did not recognise them." He sent another servant; the cultivators beat this one too. Then the master sent his son; he said: "Perhaps they will respect my son." But since they knew that he was heir to the vineyard, these cultivators seized him and killed him. He who has ears to hear, let him hear!'

This is a form of the parable of the vineyard, found in Mark 12. 1–8 and parallels (Matthew 21. 33–39; Luke 20. 9–15).

Saying 66
Jesus said: 'Show me the stone which the builders rejected; that is the corner-stone.'

In all three Synoptic Gospels the parable of the vineyard is followed by the quotation of Psalm 118. 22: 'The stone which the builders rejected has become head of the corner' (i.e. top of the pediment). The point is that Christ, rejected by the leaders of Israel, is exalted by God (cf. Acts 4. 11). Here no reference is made to its being an Old Testament quotation. Hippolytus tells us that the Naassenes spoke of the archetypal heavenly Man (whom they called Adamas) as 'the chief corner stone'.[45]

Saying 67
Jesus said: 'He who knows the All and has no need but of himself, has need everywhere.'

[45] *Refutation* v. 7. 35. For Adamas cf. p. 118, n. 22.

This saying may have had a meaning, but its meaning has eluded most commentators. Perhaps it has suffered corruption in the course of transmission. In Saying 77 Jesus himself is 'the All'.

Saying 68

Jesus said: 'Happy are you when you are hated and persecuted, and find no place there where you have been persecuted.'

This is based on Luke 6. 22 and Matthew 5. 11. The end of the saying is obscure.

Saying 69

Jesus said: 'Happy are those who have been persecuted in heart. It is they who have come to know the Father. Happy are those who are hungry, because they will be filled and satisfied.'

The first part of this saying is to the same effect as Saying 68; the promise that the persecuted ones will know the Father is similar to the canonical promise that pure in heart will see God (Matthew 5. 8). The beatitude pronounced on the hungry is based on Luke 6. 21a (Matthew 5. 6 amplifies it to apply to 'those who hunger and thirst for righteousness').

Saying 70

Jesus said: 'When you bring forth that which is within yourselves, what you have will save you. If you have not that within yourselves, what you have not within you will kill you.'

This Gnosticising variant of Saying 41 may refer to the heavenly light, which is the salvation of those who possess it but the destruction of those who lack it.

Saying 71

Jesus said: 'I will destroy this house and no one will be able to build it again.'

This saying begins like that ascribed to Jesus by the 'false witnesses' at his trial (Mark 14. 58; cf. John 2. 19), but it ends with a denial of any possibility of rebuilding. Continuity between the old order and the new is ruled out.

Saying 72
[A man] said to him: 'Tell my brothers to share my father's property with me.' He said to him: 'Man, who made me a distributor?' Then, turning to his disciples, he said: 'May I never be a distributor!'

This is parallel to the conversation of Luke 12. 13 f., which precedes the parable of the rich fool (cf. Saying 63).

Saying 73
Jesus said: 'The harvest is great but the labourers are few. Pray the Lord to send labourers into the harvest.'

Parallel to Luke 10. 2 and Matthew 9. 37 f.

Saying 74
He said: 'Lord, there are many around the opening but no one in the well.'

This appears to be said by one of the disciples to Jesus. The well is the well of truth: many approach it without getting into it. Celsus, the anti-Christian writer of the second century, quotes the saying (in Greek) from the *Heavenly Dialogue* of the Ophite Gnostics.[46]

Saying 75
Jesus said: 'Many stand outside at the door, but it is only the single ones who enter the bridal chamber.'

This is another variation on the theme 'Many are called but few are chosen' (Matthew 22. 14). The 'bridal chamber' figures

---

[46] As quoted by Origen, *Against Celsus* viii. 16. For the general idea compare Saying 23 (p. 124). The form is similar to that of a Greek mystery-saying quoted by Plato: 'The wand-bearers are many, but the initiates are few' (*Phaedo* 69c).

in several Gnostic texts as the place where the soul is reunited with its proper element; it is accessible only to the 'single' (in the sense of Sayings 4, 49).[47] There is a superficial resemblance to the parable of the ten virgins (Matthew 25. 1–13), but there it is to the wedding feast, not to the bridal chamber, that the wise virgins are admitted. (Cf. Saying 104.)

Saying 76
Jesus said: 'The kingdom of the Father is like a merchant who had a load (of merchandise) and found a pearl. That merchant was a wise man; he sold the load (of merchandise) and bought the one pearl. Do you also seek for the imperishable treasure which endures, where no moth enters to devour it nor does the worm destroy it.'

This is parallel to the parable of the pearl of great price in Matthew 13. 45 f. In this version the pearl is probably the true knowledge, as in the beautiful *Hymn of the Pearl* preserved in the Syriac *Acts of Thomas*.[48] The admonition which follows the parable is based on Luke 12. 33 (cf. Matthew 6. 20).

Saying 77
Jesus said: 'I am the light which shines upon all. I am the All; All has gone forth from me and All has come back to me. Cleave the wood, and there am I; raise the stone, and there you will find me.'

Jesus is not only the light of the world (cf. John 1. 9; 8. 12); all things cohere in him (Colossians 1. 17) and he embodies the fulness of deity (cf. Colossians 2. 9). This is presented here in pantheistic terms going far beyond the sense of such a canonical

[47] The Valentinian Gnostics observed a sacrament of the bridal chamber, through which light was received. According to the *Gospel of Philip* (a Valentinian collection of sayings identified, like the *Gospel of Thomas*, among the Nag Hammadi papyri), 'if any one becomes a son of the bridal chamber, he will receive the light; if any one does not receive it while he is in this place, he will not receive it in the other place' (Saying 127). Cf. p. 154, n. 60.

[48] This hymn is an allegorical account of the soul going on a journey to Egypt for the sake of the one pearl; F. C. Burkitt called it 'the most noble poem of Christian antiquity' and added that 'it is worth while to learn Syriac, so as to be able to read it in the original' (*Early Christianity outside the Roman Empire* [London, 1899], p. 61).

saying as Matthew 18. 20. For the light cf. Sayings 24 and 50. In the Greek text of P. Oxy. 1. 4 the words 'Raise the stone, and there you will find me; cleave the wood, and there am I' are appended to what appears in this collection as Saying 30.

Saying 78
Jesus said: 'Why did you go out to the open country? Was it to see a reed shaken by the wind, or to see a man dressed in fine clothes? [No; such persons are found in the houses of] your kings and magnates: they are so dressed, but they do not know the truth.'

In the canonical tradition similar words are spoken with reference to John the Baptist (Luke 7. 24 f.; Matthew 11. 7 f.). Here the reference to John is lost (see Saying 46) and the saying serves to point a contrast between being well-to-do and knowing the truth.

Saying 79
In the crowd a woman said to him: 'Happy the womb that gave you birth and the breasts that suckled you!' He said to her: 'Happy are those who have heard the Father's word and keep it in truth. The days will come when you will say: "Happy the womb that never gave birth and the breasts that never suckled children!"'

Two quite independent sayings are conflated here. Jesus's reply to the woman who says how wonderful it must be to be his mother indicates that to do the will of God is more wonderful still (Luke 11. 27 f.), but this is merged with his words to the weeping woman on the Via Dolorosa (Luke 23. 29). The two sayings are linked by the common theme of bearing and suckling children, but the historical perspective of the second (the impending siege and capture of Jerusalem in A.D. 70) is here replaced by a suggestion that motherhood is incompatible with 'hearing the Father's word and keeping it in truth'. As regularly (except in Saying 100), 'God' in the canonical text is here replaced by 'the Father'.

Saying 80
Jesus said: 'He who has come to know the world has fallen into the body; and as for him who has fallen into the body, the world is not worthy of him.'

This is practically identical with Saying 56, except for the use of 'body' in place of 'corpse' (see p. 135).

Saying 81
Jesus said: 'Let him who has acquired riches become a king, and let him who has power renounce it.'

This saying either disparages material wealth and power, or commends true wealth and power in the spiritual realm (cf. Saying 2); he who has the latter will renounce the world. See Saying 110.

Saying 82
Jesus said: 'He who is near me is near the fire, and he who is far from me is far from the kingdom.'

This was known to Origen (A.D. 185–254), who could not be sure whether it was a genuine saying of Jesus or not.[49] The fire is a symbol of the 'kingdom of the Father' (cf. Sayings 10, 16). We may recall that, according to Justin Martyr and others, a fire was kindled on Jordan when Jesus was baptised.[50]

Saying 83
Jesus said: 'Images appear to man, but the light which is in them is hidden in the image of the Father's light. He will reveal himself; his image is concealed by his light.'

The 'image of the Father's light' is presumably Christ (cf. 2 Corinthians 4. 4; Colossians 1. 15), who cannot be adequately

---

[49] *Homilies on Jeremiah* 20. 3. Origen perhaps knew that it came from the *Gospel of Thomas*, but in view of his rejection of the *Gospel of Thomas* as apocryphal (*Homilies on Luke*, on 1. 1), he may not have felt free to quote explicitly from it with apparent approval.

[50] Justin Martyr, *Dialogue with Trypho* 88. 3: 'When Jesus went down into the water a fire was kindled in the Jordan.' Cf. the 'light' which shone on the same occasion according to the *Gospel of the Ebionites* (p. 107).

perceived by those who are still in mortal body. When mortality is at last sloughed off, he will be fully manifest (cf. Colossians 3. 4; 1 John 3. 2). Cf. Saying 50.

Saying 84
Jesus said: 'When you see your likeness, you rejoice. But when you see your images which came into being before you, which neither die nor become manifest, how much will you endure?'

This carries on the thought of the previous saying. Since men are created in the divine image (Genesis 1. 26 f.), Christ, who is himself the divine image, is the archetypal man, the true Adam.

Saying 85
Jesus said: 'Adam came into being from great power and great wealth, and he was not worthy of you. For if he had been worthy, [he would] not [have tasted] death.'

Adam was created in the divine image, yet he sinned and involved his race in mortality. For 'great wealth' cf. Saying 29.

Saying 86
Jesus said: '[The foxes] have earths and the birds have nests, but the Son of Man has no place to lay his head and rest.'

This is parallel to Luke 9. 58 and Matthew 8. 20. True rest is not to be found in this world (cf. Sayings 50, 51, 90).

Saying 87
Jesus said: 'Wretched is the body which depends on a body, and wretched is the soul which depends on them both.'

This cryptic saying (cf. Saying 112) disparages the mortal body, which is given birth from another body. It is best for the soul to be as independent as possible of bodily life.

Saying 88
Jesus said: 'The angels and the prophets will come to you and

give you what is yours. As for you, give them what is in your hands, and say to yourselves: "On what day will they come and take what is theirs?"'

The question at the end is reminiscent of the message received by the rich fool in Luke 12. 20: 'This night your soul is required of you' (cf. Saying 63). On the day when mortal life ends the heavenly messengers give men their proper heritage (the kingdom of the Father).

Saying 89
Jesus said: 'Why do you wash the outside of the cup? Do you not understand that he who made the inside is also he who made the outside?'

This saying, reproduced from Luke 11. 39 f., is directed against those who pay attention to external rites more than to inward purity.

Saying 90
Jesus said: 'Come to me, for my yoke is easy and my rule is gentle, and you will find rest for yourselves.'

This saying is a somewhat compressed parallel to the 'wisdom' logion Matthew 11. 28-30 (cf. Saying 58 for a more remote parallel).

Saying 91
They said to him: 'Tell us who you are, so that we may believe in you.' He said to them: 'You discern the face of the sky and of the earth, but you have not known that which is before your face, and you do not know how to discern this time.'

The disciples' request is similar to that of the man cured of his blindness in John 9. 36 (cf. John 8. 25-30); Jesus's answer is based on his words in Luke 12. 54-56, but in this context the original historical reference has been replaced by an exhortation to self-knowledge.

Saying 92
Jesus said: 'Seek and you will find. But the things about
which you asked me at that time I did not tell you then; now,
when I desire to tell them, you do not enquire after them.'

The first sentence comes from Luke 11. 9 and Matthew 7. 7.
The distinction between 'then' and 'now' is that between
Jesus's ministry on earth and his present exaltation to the
heavenly realm.[51] He complains that in the meantime his
disciples' interest in higher things has waned. (Cf. Saying 38.)

Saying 93
[Jesus said:] 'Do not give what is holy to the dogs, lest they
cast it on the dung-heap. Do not cast pearls before swine,
lest they make it . . .'

This saying, defective at the end, is based on Matthew 7. 6;
it implies that spiritual mysteries must not be imparted to those
who are unable to appreciate them.

Saying 94
Jesus [said]: 'He who seeks will find, and to him who
knocks it will be opened.'

In its canonical context (Luke 11. 10; Matthew 7. 8) this is
the sequel to the first part of Saying 92.

Saying 95
[Jesus said:] 'If you have money, do not lend at interest, but
give it to him from whom you will not receive it back.'

This is to the same effect as Luke 6. 34 f. (cf. Luke 14. 12–14).[52]

Saying 96
Jesus [said]: 'The kingdom of the Father is like a woman who
took a little leaven, hid it in dough, and made large loaves of
it. He who has ears to hear, let him hear!'

[51] See p. 112 with n. 7.
[52] Contrast the end of Saying 109 where, however, the lender is not
necessarily commended.

A version of the parable of Luke 13. 20 f. and Matthew 13. 33.

Saying 97
Jesus said: 'The kingdom of the Father is like a woman carrying a jar full of meal and walking along a long road. The handle of the jar broke, and the meal poured out behind her on the road without her knowing it or being able to do anything about it. When she reached home, she set down the jar and found that it was empty.'

Here is a parable of the kingdom which has no canonical parallel. The point seems to be a warning against self-confidence, against thinking that one possesses the saving knowledge when in fact it has trickled away.

Saying 98
Jesus said: 'The kingdom of the Father is like a man who wishes to kill a magnate. In his own house he unsheathes his sword and thrusts it into the wall to make sure that his hand will be steady; then he kills his victim.'

This parable, also unparalleled in the canonical tradition, may have come down from a period when Zealot activity gave it contemporary relevance. The point seems to be that any one who embarks on a costly or dangerous enterprise must first make sure that he has the necessary resources to carry it out.[53] There may be a link with the strong man whose house is ransacked in Saying 35.

Saying 99
The disciples said to him: 'Your brothers and your mother are standing outside.' He said to them: 'Those here who do my Father's will, they are my brothers and my mother; it is they who will enter my Father's kingdom.'

This saying, parallel to Mark 3. 31–35 and Matthew 12. 46–50, inculcates the same independent attitude to one's natural family as Sayings 16 and 55 (see also Saying 101).

[53] This is the point of the canonical saying in Luke 14. 28–32.

Saying 100
Jesus was shown a gold coin and was told: 'Caesar's people are demanding the taxes from us.' He said to them, 'Give Caesar what is Caesar's; give God what is God's; and give me what is mine!'

This is the incident of the tribute money recorded in Mark 12. 13–17 and parallels,[54] but the historical setting is a thing of the past and the silver denarius has become a *gold* coin. What is specially important, however, is the addition of 'give me what is mine' to the canonical saying. 'God', who is thus placed higher than Caesar but lower than Jesus, is not the Supreme Being who is always called the Father in the *Gospel of Thomas*, but the demiurge, the creator of the material world. Like Caesar, he must receive his due, but it is more important to give Jesus, the unique revealer, *his* due.

Saying 101
[Jesus said:] 'He who does not hate his father and mother in my way cannot be my disciple. And he who does [not] love his [father] and mother in my way cannot be my disciple. For my mother . . . but in truth she gave me life.'

This (unfortunately defective) saying insists, like Sayings 55 and 99, that it is spiritual relationships that really matter (cf. Luke 14. 26; Matthew 10. 37).

Saying 102
Jesus said: 'Woe to them, the Pharisees, because they are like a dog lying on a pile of fodder: he will not eat of it himself and will not allow anyone else to eat it.'

The point of this saying is the same as that of Saying 39, where the Pharisees and scribes are criticised for impounding the keys of knowledge; but here it is expressed in terms of Aesop's fable of the dog in the manger.

Saying 103
Jesus said: 'Happy is the man who knows in which part of

[54] Cf. the presentation of this incident in Egerton Papyrus 2 (p. 162).

the night robbers will come in, so that he may rise and collect his [strength] and gird his loins before they come in.'

This is parallel to Luke 12. 39 and Matthew 24. 43; the moral is 'Be prepared!'—but not for the same contingency as that envisaged in the original setting.

Saying 104
They said: 'Come, let us pray and fast today.' Jesus said: 'What sin have I committed, or what omission am I guilty of? When the bridegroom comes forth from the bridal chamber, one never fasts or prays then.'

This saying expresses the same negative attitude to external acts of piety as Sayings 6, 14 and 27. It is similar to Jesus's reply to the criticism of his disciples for not fasting in Mark 2. 18–20, but prayer is here added to fasting. The canonical mention of the bridegroom, which is purely parabolic, is amplified here by reference to the bridal chamber, which (as we have said in the comment on Saying 75) played an important part in the special vocabulary of some Gnostic groups. The opening words of Jesus's reply ('What sin have I committed . . . ?') resemble his reply in the *Gospel according to the Hebrews* that he should join his family in seeking baptism at John's hands.[55]

Saying 105
Jesus said: 'He who knows father and mother will be called the son of a harlot.'

The point of this saying may be quite problematical. It may imply the denial that Jesus entered the world by such a supposedly unworthy manner as being born of woman. On the other hand, Jesus may be complaining that he himself, who knows his true Father to be God (cf. John 8. 18 ff.)—and possibly his true mother to be the Holy Spirit, as in the *Gospel according to Hebrews*[56]—is nevertheless stigmatised as being

[55] See p. 100.
[56] See p. 101.

'born of fornication' (according to a probably mistaken interpretation of John 8. 41).[57]

Saying 106
Jesus said: 'When you make the two one, you will become
sons of man, and if you say, "Move over, mountain!" it will
move.'

When the two sexes are reunited in a single personality, true
manhood will be achieved; for this doctrine see Sayings 4, 11,
22. For mountain-moving faith cf. Saying 48.

Saying 107
Jesus said: 'The kingdom is like a shepherd who had a
hundred sheep. One of them, the biggest, wandered away.
He left the ninety-nine others and searched for this single
sheep until he found it. After taking this trouble, he said
to the sheep: "I love you more than the ninety-nine
others!"'

In the canonical versions of the parable of the lost sheep
(Luke 15. 3–7; cf. Matthew 18. 12 f.), the owner puts himself to
exceptional trouble over the hundredth sheep just because it is
lost. This is unacceptable to our present editor, who rationalises
the situation by explaining that the lost sheep was the biggest
(and presumably the most valuable) in the flock. Either the
shepherd is Jesus and the hundredth sheep the true Gnostic,
or the shepherd is the Gnostic and the sheep the true knowledge
(like the big fish in Saying 8 and the pearl in Saying 76).

Saying 108
Jesus said: 'He who drinks from my mouth will become as I
am, and I myself will become he, and the hidden things will
be revealed to him.'

[57] The Jews' protest in John 8. 41 ('we were not born of fornication')
arises from their suspicion that Jesus was repeating Samaritan calumnies
about the origin of the Jewish people (cf. verse 48, 'you are a Samaritan').
Calumnies about Jesus's parentage, though not implied in John 8. 41, 48,
were later current; see pp. 57, 175.

To drink from Jesus's mouth is to imbibe his teaching: he who does this perfectly becomes one with Jesus. The figure of drinking the water that Jesus supplies is used in a different sense in John 4. 14; 7. 37.

Saying 109
Jesus said: 'The kingdom is like a man who had a treasure hidden in his field, without knowing of it. When he died, he left it [the field] to his son, who also knew nothing [of the treasure]. When he inherited that field, he sold it; and the man who bought it found the treasure while he was ploughing. Then he began to lend money at interest to whomsoever he pleased.'

This version of the parable of the hidden treasure (cf. Matthew 13. 44) has a novel ending. The treasure, like the pearl in Saying 76, is the true knowledge; if those who have this within their grasp do not avail themselves of it, it will pass to others who will profit by it.

Saying 110
Jesus said: 'He who has found the world and acquired riches, let him renounce the world.'

This seems to be a variation on Saying 81 (cf. also Saying 56).

Saying 111
Jesus said: 'The heavens will be rolled up, and the earth, before your eyes, and he who draws his life from the Living One will not see death; for Jesus says: "As for him who finds himself, the world is not worthy of him."'

That the believer will outlast the material universe is a commonplace of the Old and New Testaments (cf. Isaiah 54. 10). The words with which the saying opens are similar to those of Revelation 6. 14 (drawn from Isaiah 34. 4) and 2 Peter 3. 10–12. The assurance that 'he who draws his life from the Living One will not see death' echoes Saying 1. For the closing words cf. the end of Saying 56.

Saying 112

Jesus said: 'Woe to the flesh which depends on the soul; woe to the soul which depends on the flesh!'

This seems to teach the same lesson as Saying 87 (there we find 'body' where here we find 'flesh').

Saying 113

His disciples said to him: 'When will the kingdom come?' [Jesus said:] 'It will not come when it is expected. They will not say "See, here it is!" or "See, there it is!" – but the kingdom of the Father is spread abroad on the earth and men do not see it.'

This is a variant of the question and answer in Luke 17. 20 f., though there the question is asked by the Pharisees, not by the disciples. Whatever is meant by the answer in Luke 17. 21, 'the kingdom of God is in the midst of you' (or 'within you', or 'within your grasp'),[58] in the *Gospel of Thomas* the kingdom is no longer to be understood in the historical context of Jesus's ministry; it has lost its eschatological implication and is given a universal reference.

Saying 114

Simon Peter said to them: 'Let Mary depart from our midst, because women are not worthy of the [true] life.' Jesus said: 'See, I will so draw her as to make her a man, in order that she may become a living spirit like you men. For every woman who becomes a man will enter into the kingdom of heaven.'

This is not the only place in Gnostic literature where Peter expresses impatience at the presence of Mary Magdalene in their entourage.[59] The general rabbinic idea that women were

[58] Cf. Saying 3a (p. 113).

[59] In *Pistis Sophia*, when Mary has expounded the 'mystery of repentance' in a Gnostic sense and been congratulated by Jesus for her insight, Peter protests: 'My Lord, we are not able to bear with this woman, speaking instead of us; she has not let any of us speak but speaks often herself' (54b). In the John Rylands University Library of Manchester there is an early third-century Greek papyrus fragment (P. Ryl. 463) of a *Gospel according to Mary* (*Magdalene*), in which the disciples discuss revelations which the Saviour is said to have given exclusively to Mary. Peter is unwilling to

incapable of appreciating religious doctrine — compare the disciples' astonishment at Jacob's well when they found Jesus 'talking with a woman' (John 4. 27) — was reinforced in Gnostic anthropology, where woman was a secondary and defective being. Yet none could deny Mary's fidelity: to an objective observer, it surpassed that of the male disciples. Jesus's promise that she will become a man, so as to gain admittance to the kingdom of heaven, envisages the reintegration of the original order, when Adam was created male and female (Genesis 1. 27). Adam was 'the man' as much before the removal of Eve from his side as after (Genesis 2. 18–25). Therefore, when the primal unity is restored and death is abolished, man will still be man (albeit more perfectly so), but woman will no longer be woman; she will be reabsorbed into man.[60]

On this note, which was probably regarded as of high importance for the understanding of man's place in the universe, the compilation ends; there follows the colophon: 'The Gospel according to Thomas'.

The sayings of Jesus are best to be understood in the light of the historical circumstances in which they were spoken. Only when we have understood them thus can we safely endeavour to recognise the permanent truth which they convey. When they are detached from their original historical setting and arranged in an anthology, their interpretation is more precarious. The *Gospel of Thomas* was probably not the first collection of sayings of Jesus ever to be compiled; a mid-first-century collection of his sayings is widely held to have provided one among several sources for the Gospels of Matthew and Luke.[61] When the sayings are detached from their historical

believe that the Saviour would have committed privately to a woman truths which he did not impart to his male disciples, but Levi rebukes him and defends Mary. (Part of the same work survives in a Coptic version in the Berlin papyrus 8502.) For Mary cf. Saying 21 (p. 122).

[60] This is the point of the mystery of the bridal chamber (cf. Saying 75, p. 141); it was a form of initiation calculated to reverse the process by which death entered. 'When Eve was in Adam, there was no death; but when she was separated from him, death came into being' (*Gospel of Philip* 71). See Appendix (p. 157).

[61] The collection commonly designated 'Q'.

setting, they tend to be interpreted in another context, and this context will be determined by the conscious beliefs and unconscious presuppositions of the community in which they circulate in this form. In the New Testament itself we have evidence not only of what the sayings of Jesus meant in the situation of his ministry but also of how they were understood some decades later in the early church.

For the most part, the interpretation of the sayings collected in the *Gospel of Thomas* is not explicit but is left to be inferred. It is reasonably plain, however, that their interpretation was controlled by the Gnostic or quasi-Gnostic views of the groups for which they were compiled and in which they circulated. As the historical and geographical setting — Palestine under the Romans and the Herods around A.D. 30 — has been almost entirely forgotten, the sayings are treated as expressions of timeless truth. The kingdom which Jesus proclaimed is no longer the new order which was breaking into the world to replace the Gentile empires but that universally present realm into which the recipient of the true knowledge withdraws from the evanescent pressures of the material world. Jesus himself is pre-eminently the revealer of the true knowledge to those who are able to receive it. No collection of sayings of Jesus can properly be called a Gospel because by its nature it has no passion narrative, and the passion narrative is the core of the essential gospel. But least of all can this collection be called a Gospel because not only does it lack a passion narrative but it includes only one saying (55) remotely hinting at the passion.

The main thrust of the *Gospel of Thomas* was met in advance by the author of the First Epistle of John, who announces at the outset that he is about to share with his readers all that he and his companions had experienced personally of the gospel story — 'the message of life'. The true knowledge, he insists, is accessible to all his readers without distinction — children, young men, and fathers — instead of being confined to a spiritual élite, as some other teachers claimed. 'You, no less than they', he tells them, 'are among the initiated; this is the gift of the Holy One, and by it you all have knowledge' (1 John 2. 20, N.E.B.). This initiation into the true knowledge is the anointing of the Spirit by which they are bound together with God in the fellowship of that love which was perfectly revealed in the self-sacrifice of Christ. 'It is by this that we know what love is: that Christ laid down his life for us. And we in our turn are bound to lay down our lives for our brothers' (1 John 3. 16). It is the absence of this note of self-sacrificing love from the *Gospel of Thomas* that, more than anything else, distinguishes it from the earlier gospel tradition.

APPENDIX TO CHAPTER SEVEN

The *Gospel according to the Egyptians*, a Greek work, was a thoroughly Gnostic production; according to Hippolytus (*Refutation* v. 8), it was used by the Naassenes. Clement of Alexandria (*c.* A.D. 180) quotes from it an alleged saying of Jesus, 'I came to destroy the works of the female', and illustrates it by a conversation between Jesus and Salome, reported in the same Gospel. When Salome asked him, 'How long will death prevail?' she received the reply: 'As long as you women bear children.' 'Then', said she, 'I have done well in bearing no children.' (Can this Salome be the mother of the sons of Zebedee?) 'Eat every herb,' said the Lord, 'but not that which has a bitter fruit.' When she pressed her original question again, he answered more fully: 'When you trample on the garment of shame, when the two become one and the male with the female neither male nor female' (*Miscellanies* iii. 45, 63 ff., 91).

Death, it was realised, is bound up in the same process as conception and birth. So long as conception and birth take place, death will prevail. Conception and birth are 'the works of the female' and so, indirectly, therefore is death, which Jesus, according to the New Testament, came to abolish (1 Corinthians 15. 26; 2 Timothy 1. 10). There was a time in human history when death did not prevail: that was before Eve was separated from Adam, according to Genesis 2. 21–23. At that time, of course, conception and birth played no part in human life. Therefore, it was argued, if woman is reabsorbed in man, there will be no more conception and birth, and equally no more death. In some Gnostic groups there was a 'sacrament of the bridal chamber' which anticipated this return to the original androgynous state (see Sayings 75, 104, and p. 154 with n. 60). Other possible affinities to the *Gospel according to the Egyptians* occur in Sayings 4, 11 and especially 22.

Clement of Alexandria takes the words of Jesus to Salome seriously but, refusing to endorse their *prima facie* disapproval of marriage and parenthood, replaces their Gnostic significance with an ethical allegorisation. So does the author of the mid-second-century homily traditionally misnamed the Second Epistle of Clement: 'the Lord himself, when asked by someone when his kingdom would come, said: "When two shall be one and the outside as the inside, and the male with the female neither male nor female." Now "the two are one" when we tell one another the truth . . . "The outside as the inside" means: . . . just as your body is visible, so let your soul also be manifest in your good works. And "the male with the female neither male nor female" means that when a brother sees a sister [i.e. a fellow-Christian of the other sex] he should not think of her as female nor she of him as male. When you do this, he means, the kingdom of my Father will come' (2 Clement 12. 2–6).

Chapter Eight

More Uncanonical Scriptures

Another Oxyrhynchus Papyrus

SOME time after the discovery of the Oxyrhynchus sayings of Jesus mentioned in our last chapter, another papyrus came to light (P. Oxy. 840)[1] containing what looked like a fragment of an apocryphal Gospel. The lost section immediately preceding what remains at the beginning of the fragment evidently recorded the fate of some people who are adduced by way of warning to Jesus's hearers (cf. Luke 13. 1–5). After the last words of a mutilated sentence ('. . . before he does wrong he makes all kinds of ingenious excuses') the fragment proceeds:

'But take care lest you also suffer the same things as they did, for men who do evil not only receive their chastisement among the living but they await punishment and much torment.' Then he took them and brought them into the place of purification itself, and was walking in the temple. A Pharisee, a chief priest named Levi, met them and said to the Saviour: 'Who gave you leave to tread this place of purification and see these holy vessels when you have not bathed and your disciples have not washed their feet? But you have trodden this temple in a state of defilement, whereas no one else treads it or dares to view these holy vessels without having bathed and changed his clothes.' Thereupon the Saviour stood with his disciples and answered him: 'Are you then clean, here in the temple as you are?' 'Yes', said he, 'I am clean, for I have bathed in the pool of David and have gone down by one staircase and come up by another, and I have put on clean white clothes. Then I came and looked at the holy vessels.' 'Alas', said the Saviour, 'you blind men who cannot see! You have washed in this water which

[1] *Oxyrhynchus Papyri*, Vol. 5 (1908).

pours forth here, in which dogs and pigs have wallowed night and day, and you have washed and scrubbed your outer skin, which harlots and flute-girls also anoint and wash and scrub, beautifying themselves to arouse human desire, while inwardly they are filled with scorpions and all un-righteousness. But my disciples and I, whom you charge with not having bathed, have bathed ourselves in the living water which comes down from heaven.'

Readers of the canonical Gospels are familiar with Jesus's repeated insistence that in the religious sphere it is inward purification, not external washing, that is important (cf. Mark 7. 1–23); and that is the point of this extract. It may be regarded, more particularly, as an expansion of Matthew 23. 25 f. into the form of a narrative. The circumstantiality of the references to the temple and its installations might convey an impression of verisimilitude to readers who knew little or nothing about them, but they betray the imagination of a period later than the destruction of the temple and have little in common with what we know of the temple and its ordinances as they actually were.[2] The 'place of purification' cannot be identified, and laymen like Jesus and his disciples had no opportunity of looking at the 'holy vessels' (by which the furniture in the sanctuary itself is probably meant). Most grotesque of all is the suggestion that 'pigs' wallowed in the water in which the temple staff or visitors washed, whereas their presence would not be tolerated in any Jewish community. The reference to 'harlots and flute-girls' has been thought to point to the *Gospel according to the Hebrews* as the source of the extract, since they are mentioned together in the version of the parable of the talents ascribed to that Gospel.[3] But this is a very slender argument.

Egerton Papyrus 2

In the summer of 1934 the British Museum acquired a collection of papyri including some fragments of a codex, apparently of a life of Christ or something similar, which

---

[2] Our two most important sources of knowledge about the Jerusalem temple in New Testament times are the description in Josephus, *War* v. 184–287, and another, based on reliable oral tradition, in the Mishnah tractate *Middoth*.

[3] See p. 103.

attracted attention because of its early date, not later than
A.D. 150. The papyri were assigned by the Museum to the
Egerton Collection, and the fragmentary codex is accordingly
catalogued as Egerton Papyrus 2. The scholars who first studied
the fragments concluded that they belonged to a previously
unknown Gospel. The discovery was announced by H. Idris
Bell, Keeper of Manuscripts, in *The Times* of January 23, 1935,
under a caption 'A New Gospel'; and the full text was published
by the Trustees of the Museum later that year in a volume
entitled *Fragments of an Unknown Gospel and Other Early
Christian Papyri*, edited by H. I. Bell and T. C. Skeat.

The fragments come from four separate incidents, which are
reproduced below in the order given them in the first edition:

1. [And Jesus said] to the lawyers: '[Punish] every wrong-
doer and transgressor, and not me . . .' Then, turning to the
rulers of the people, he spoke this word: 'You search the
scriptures, in which you think you have life; it is they that
bear witness to me. Do not think that I have come to accuse
you to my Father; it is Moses who accuses you, on whom you
have set your hope.' When they said, 'We know well that God
spoke to Moses; but as for you, we do not know where you
come from', Jesus said in reply: 'Now your unbelief is
exposed . . .'. . . . [They gave counsel] to the crowd to
collect stones and stone him. The rulers sought to lay their
hands on him in order to arrest him and hand him over to the
crowd; but they could not arrest him, because the hour of his
betrayal had not yet come. The Lord himself, passing out
through their midst, escaped them.

The Johannine affinities of this passage are evident. Jesus's
words to the rulers of the people are practically identical with his
words in John 5. 39, 45. Their reply to him is based on the
Pharisees' words in John 9. 29 to the blind man whom Jesus
had cured. The plot to stone Jesus is paralleled in John 8. 59
and 10. 31. For the attempt to arrest him we may compare
John 7. 30: 'they sought to arrest him; but no one laid hands on
him, because his hour had not yet come' (cf. 10. 39: 'Again they
tried to arrest him, but he escaped their hands'). The secondary
nature of the papyrus text is evident (among other things) from

its effort to clarify, with a reference to Jesus's betrayal, the somewhat cryptic Johannine clause: 'his hour had not yet come'.[4]

2. And see, a leper approached him and said: 'Teacher Jesus, while journeying with lepers and eating with them in the inn, I myself also became a leper. If, therefore, you are willing, I am cleansed.' The Lord said to him: 'I am willing: be cleansed.' And immediately the leprosy departed from him, and the Lord said: 'Go, show yourself to the priests . . .'

This incident follows straight on from the preceding one on the papyrus but, far from sharing its Johannine features, it is clearly a reproduction of the healing of the leper narrated in Mark 1. 40–45, with a little additional human interest in the leper's account of how he contracted leprosy. (We may compare the similar amplification of the story of the man with the withered hand in the *Gospel according to the Hebrews*.)[5]

3. Coming to him to put him to the proof, they tested him, saying: 'Teacher Jesus, we know that you have come from God, for the things which you do bear witness beyond all the prophets. Tell us then: Is it lawful to render to kings what pertains to their rule? Shall we render it to them or not?' But Jesus, knowing their mind, said to them in indignation: 'Why do you call me teacher with your mouth, when you do not listen to what I say? Well did Isaiah prophesy of you when he said: "This people honours me with its lips, but their heart is far from me; in vain do they worship me, [teaching as doctrines merely human] commandments."'

This extract combines the beginning of the Synoptic narrative about the tribute money (Mark 12. 13–15a) with part of the debate about eating with unwashed hands (Mark 7. 6 f., quoting Isaiah 29. 13).[6] The latter passage amplifies Jesus's response in Mark 12. 15b to the question about the tribute:

[4] Cf. John 2. 4; 7. 30; 8. 20. The 'hour' is the hour of his passion, presented in the Fourth Gospel as his glorification.
[5] See pp. 101 f.
[6] The questioners' opening words also echo Nicodemus's approach in John 3. 2.

'But knowing their hypocrisy, he said to them, "Why put me to the test?"' The conflation of two separate passages is proof enough in itself of the secondary character of the extract, but its secondary character is underlined by the changes from the Synoptic wording of the question. We have seen how Saying 100 in the *Gospel of Thomas* deviates from the Synoptic form of the incident, but at least it preserves the reference to Caesar.[7] Here the question has been completely generalised. The Synoptic form is true to the life-setting in Jesus's Jerusalem ministry, where the propriety of Jews' paying tribute to Caesar, a pagan monarch, was a burning religious and political issue. But now the question concerns the principle of paying kings in general 'what pertains to their rule', of rendering, in Paul's words, 'tribute to whom tribute is due' (Romans 13. 7); and the original point, in its Judaean context of A.D. 30, is lost.

4. The remaining fragment has neither Synoptic nor Johannine parallels. Unfortunately it is full of lacunae and impossible of restoration to anything like its original state. Jesus apparently asks a question about something which has been

'... enclosed in its place, ... placed below invisibly, ... its weight immeasurable'. ... And when they were perplexed at his strange question, Jesus as he walked stood on the bank of Jordan and, stretching out his right hand, filled it [with seed] and sowed it on the river. Then ... [? he blessed] the water which had been sown [with seed] ... in their presence and it produced much fruit ... to their joy (?) ...

There may be a vague echo here of the grain of wheat which, in Jesus's words in John 12. 24, 'bears much fruit' only if it 'falls into the earth and dies'[8] — but the sowing of seed on the water is far removed from sowing it in the earth. We seem here to have an extravagant miracle story from an apocryphal Gospel; had more of the story survived, it might have proved to contain

[7] See p. 149.
[8] C. H. Dodd tentatively restored Jesus's opening question along these lines: 'When a husbandman has enclosed a small seed in a secret place, so that it is invisibly buried, how does its abundance become immeasurable?' (*New Testament Studies* [Manchester U.P., 1953], p. 43).

some allegorical significance – possibly along the lines of Ecclesiastes 11. 1: 'Cast your bread upon the waters, for you will find it after many days.' Or possibly some baptismal teaching might be involved. We cannot know, in the present state of our ignorance.

What then are we to say about the document to which those fragments belong? One thing is clear: it is not a 'new Gospel' preserving traditions independent of the canonical records, as was once thought. It is a compilation by someone who knew the four canonical Gospels and at least one apocryphal Gospel. The extracts are too few and fragmentary for us to speak confidently about the nature of the work to which they belonged: it may have been an attempt to arrange the material of the Gospels in a continuous narrative, a rudimentary *Diatessaron* (or *Diapente*),[9] or it may have been a manual of instruction, designed to teach the elements of the gospel story.

A second edition of Mark?

In December 1960 Professor Morton Smith of Columbia University, New York City, reported to the ninety-sixth meeting of the American Society of Biblical Literature and Exegesis a discovery of exceptional interest.[10] While cataloguing the contents of the library of Mar Saba monastery, some twelve miles south-east of Jerusalem, in 1958 he found a hand-written copy of a letter in Greek on the end-papers of a Dutch book printed in the mid-seventeenth century.[11] The writing was in a mid-eighteenth-century hand (approximately), but the letter of which this was a copy was over a thousand years earlier. The heading of the copy runs: 'From Letters of Clement, author of the *Stromateis* [*Miscellanies*], to Theodore'.[12] The text itself, however, makes no mention either of the author or of the person or persons addressed. On stylistic grounds Professor Smith is disposed to regard the ascription of

[9] See p. 107. As *Diatessaron* means a fourfold harmony, so *Diapente* means a fivefold harmony.

[10] 'A Letter Attributed to Clement of Alexandria and Containing Quotations from a Secret Gospel Attributed to St. Mark': cf. *Journal of Biblical Literature* 80 (1961), p. iv.

[11] The book was Isaac Voss's edition of the Greek text of six of the letters of Ignatius: *Epistolae Genuinae S. Ignatii Martyris* (Amsterdam, 1646).

[12] John of Damascus (*c.* 680–760), who himself lived at Mar Saba, refers to letters of Clement of Alexandria (*Sacra Parallela* 311, 312, 313).

the letter to Clement of Alexandria as authentic; an independent judgment on this and other questions must await the publication of the text, which has unfortunately been held up thus far.

The chief interest of the letter lies in the fact that it makes reference to a longer edition of the Gospel of Mark, current at Alexandria, which included 'secret' sayings of Jesus not found in the canonical text. According to the writer of the letter, Mark came to Alexandria from Rome, where he had already published the shorter edition of his Gospel. At Alexandria he expanded it and added some 'secret' sayings. (Then the Gnostic teacher Carpocrates took this expanded text and expanded it further with spurious material of his own.)[13] The longer edition inserted after Mark 10. 34 the story of the raising of a rich young man from the tomb[14] — a story which bears some resemblance to the account of the raising of Lazarus in John 11. 1–44. Then comes the incident of James and John's request to Jesus for the places of chief honour in his kingdom (Mark 10. 35 ff.); after that there is a reference to Salome.[15]

In so far as it is possible to say anything about this report while the document remains unpublished, it may be said that this expanded Gospel of Mark bears all the signs of Gnostic editing. The 'secret' character of the additional sayings is the most obvious Gnosticising feature. The story of Mark's founding of the church of Alexandria[16] probably represents a late attempt to give an orthodox pedigree to a church which in its earliest days, or at least in the earlier part of the second century, was Gnostically inclined. Not until the later half of the second

[13] Irenaeus (*Heresies* i. 25. 5) tells us that the followers of Carpocrates (early second century) had writings in which they claimed to preserve secret teachings given by Jesus to his apostles and others, who were permitted to impart them to those who were worthy and faithful.
[14] Presumably a different person from the rich man of Mark 10. 17–22. Cf. the incident of the second rich man in the *Gospel according to the Hebrews* (see p. 103).
[15] After the first clause in Mark 10. 46 Salome is said to have been in Jericho with the young man's sister and mother, 'but Jesus did not receive them'. Salome figures prominently in apocryphal Gospel literature; see pp. 86, 137, 157.
[16] This story is preserved in Eusebius, *Hist. Eccl.* ii. 16. 1. Cf. W. Bauer, *Orthodoxy and Heresy in Earliest Christianity* (Philadelphia, 1970), pp. 44 ff.; A. A. T. Ehrhardt, *The Framework of the New Testament Stories* (Manchester U.P., 1964), pp. 174 ff.

century, when the Gnostic groups were more definitely separated from the catholic fellowship, did the Alexandrian church come under the control of a theology more in line with that of the apostolic sees of Rome and the east. When Clement or his contemporaries (c. A.D. 180) found this longer edition of Mark's Gospel preserved in Alexandria, they were willing to treat acceptable expansions as belonging to a second edition produced by Mark after his alleged coming from Rome to Alexandria, but those expansions which were manifestly Gnostic were ascribed to the school of Carpocrates.[17]

[17] Since these last three paragraphs were written, Professor Smith has published the text of the letter with a technical introduction and commentary in *Clement of Alexandria and a Secret Gospel of Mark* (Harvard University Press, 1973); he has provided a more popular account in *The Secret Gospel* (Harper and Row, New York, 1973). It would now be possible to give a better informed summary of the document than has been given above, but the study of the published text has not moved me to change my mind in any material particular. The raising of the rich young man takes place at Bethany; it is apparently a variant of the raising of Lazarus, but this young man returns to life before Jesus's arrival and cries out from the still unopened tomb. He seems to be identified with the young man of Mark 14. 51 f. who made his escape when Jesus was arrested, and possibly also with the Johannine 'disciple whom Jesus loved'.

Chapter Nine

Jesus in the Qur'ān

IN addition to the documents which we have surveyed thus far, Islamic literature and tradition make frequent reference to Jesus. Islamic literature and tradition belong to the religious movement which dates its rise from A.D. 610, the year in which Muhammad received his call at the age of forty. From a period so long after the origins of Christianity we cannot expect to find anything which will serve as independent source-material for the history of those origins. Yet the early Muslim accounts of Jesus have an interest of their own, and throw light on the form in which the gospel story first came to Muhammad's ears.

At the time of the rise of Islam Jews occupied a dominant economic position in Western Arabia, and there were many Jewish proselytes among the Arabs of that area. Christians of rival schools of thought were also active among the tribesmen in various parts of Arabia. Muhammad's first wife, Khadijah, had a Christian cousin named Waraqah, who had some knowledge of the Bible and with whom Muhammad is said to have had conversation. About the time of Muhammad's birth the Hijaz (the district in which Mecca, Muhammad's birth-place, and Medina are situated) was invaded from the Yemen by Abraha, a Christian general from Abyssinia. Muhammad was acquainted with Jews and Christians and with their sacred scriptures, called respectively the *tawrāt* (the *Torah* or Law) and the *injīl* (the *euangelion* or Gospel).

Muhammad's great controversy was with the paganism of Arabia, against which he asserted an uncompromising monotheism. It was far from his original thought to introduce a new religion: he believed that Allah,[1] who commissioned him as his messenger, was the one living and true God who had spoken

---

[1] Allah (*al-ilah*) means 'the God' (i.e. the one and only God).

through such earlier prophets as Noah, Abraham, Moses and Jesus, and that his own message was essentially theirs, bringing it to completion and applying it to the conditions of the people of Mecca and its neighbourhood. He expected that the existing 'people of the Book', the Jews and Christians, would acknowledge that his message was the truth, and was disillusioned when they found fault with it. He deplored the Jews' refusal to acknowledge Jesus as a teacher sent from God, but he also deplored the Christians' ascription to Jesus of divine honours: this, in his eyes, undermined the basic truth that God is One — 'there is no God but Allah'.

The revelations received by Muhammad are recorded in the holy book of Islam, the Qur'ān (a word which might be rendered 'recitation'). The Qur'ān comprises 114 *surahs* or chapters, and these are subdivided into verses.[2]

Jesus is regularly referred to in the Qur'ān as 'Isa ibn Maryam (Jesus son of Mary), sometimes with the additional designation al-Masih (the Messiah). The references to him are brief, apart from the account of his birth, which appears in more than one passage, from various phases of the composition of the Qur'ān.

'We[3] gave Jesus son of Mary sure signs [of his commission]', says Allah in Surah 2. 81, 'and aided him by the Holy Spirit.' Mary in her turn is set forth as an example to all believing women: 'Because Mary, daughter of 'Imran, guarded her chastity, We breathed into her womb a portion of Our Spirit; she put her trust in the words of her Lord and in his Books, and was one of the devout' (66. 12).

Maryam is the Arabic equivalent of Miriam, the Hebrew word from which we derive Greek and Latin Maria and English Mary. In the Old and New Testaments the name is borne by several women, but the most outstanding of these are Miriam the sister of Moses in the Old Testament and Mary the mother of Jesus in the New. In Surah 3 of the Qur'ān there is a sudden transition from the first to the second of these — a transition facilitated by the fact that in the Qur'ān the father of the

---

[2] Two convenient translations of the Qur'ān are by A. J. Arberry, *The Koran Interpreted* (World Classics, Oxford, 1955), and N. J. Dawood, *The Koran* (Penguin Classics, Harmondsworth, 1956).

[3] 'We' is the plural of divine majesty.

second bears the name 'Imran (Amram), as the father of the first does in the Bible (verses 30–52):

> Allah chose above all the worlds Adam and Noah, the family of Abraham and the family of 'Imran. They were all in the same line of descent. Allah is the one who hears and knows all.
>
> Remember what 'Imran's wife said: 'Lord, I dedicate to your service the child in my womb. Accept it from me. You are the one who hears and knows all.'
>
> Then, when she had given birth to the child, she said, 'Lord, I have been delivered of a girl.' Allah knew quite well what she had been delivered of; the male is not like the female. 'I have named her Mary', she continued, 'I ask you to protect her and her offspring from Satan, the accursed.'
>
> Her Lord graciously accepted her, and made her grow up a goodly child. Zechariah took charge of her. Whenever Zechariah went into the sanctuary to see her, he found food beside her. 'Mary', he said, 'how have you got this?' 'It is from Allah', she replied; 'Allah provides without stint for whomsoever he will.' Then Zechariah called on his Lord, saying: 'O my Lord, give me upright offspring; you are the hearer of prayer.' So, while he still stood praying in the sanctuary, the angels called to him, saying: 'Allah bids you rejoice concerning Yahya (John), who will confirm the word of Allah: he will be a leader, a man of abstinence, a prophet and one of the upright.' 'Lord', said he, 'how shall I have a boy, seeing I am an old man and my wife is barren?' 'So shall it be', was the reply; 'Allah does whatever he pleases.' 'My Lord', said he, 'appoint a sign for me.' He answered: 'Your sign is that you will not speak to the people for three days except by gestures. Remember your Lord at all times; give him glory in the evening and morning.'
>
> Remember also what the angels said to Mary: 'O Mary, Allah has indeed chosen you; he has purified you and exalted you above all women in the world. Be obedient to your Lord, Mary; bow down before him and worship with the worshippers.'
>
> This is an account of what is concealed, which We give to you[4] by inspiration. You were not there when they cast lots

[4] That is, to Muhammad.

with their rods to decide which of them should take charge of Mary, nor were you there when they contended about her.

The angels said, 'Mary, Allah bids you rejoice in a Word from himself, in him who is called the Messiah, Jesus son of Mary. He is eminent in this world and the next, one of those brought near to him. He will speak to men in the cradle and as a full-grown man; he will be one of the upright.' 'My Lord', said Mary, 'how shall I have a child? No man has ever touched me.' 'So shall it be', was the reply; 'Allah creates whom he pleases. Whatever he decrees, he simply says "Be!"—and it is.[5] Allah will instruct him in the Book and in Wisdom, in the Law and the Gospel;[6] he will be a messenger to the Israelites. He will say, "I come to you with a sign from your Lord. I will create for you from clay the form of a bird; I will breathe into it and by Allah's permission it will become a real bird. By Allah's permission I will heal the blind and the lepers and bring the dead to life. I will tell you what you may eat and what you may store up in your houses. That will be a sign for you if you are believers. I will confirm the Law that was before me, and make lawful some of the things which have been forbidden to you. I come to you with a sign from your Lord, so reverence Allah and obey me. Allah is my Lord and your Lord: therefore serve him. This is the straight path."'

When Jesus saw that they did not believe, he said, 'Who are my helpers[7] in the cause of Allah?' The apostles replied: 'We are Allah's helpers; we have believed in Allah. Bear witness that we have submitted ourselves to him.[8] We believe in the revelation you have sent down, O our Lord; we have followed your messenger. Write us down among the witnesses.'

They planned and Allah planned; Allah plans best. Allah said, 'Jesus, I am going to bring about your death and raise you to myself. I will separate you from the unbelievers, and exalt your followers above the unbelievers until the day of

[5] Cf. Surah 3. 52 (p. 171); 19. 36 (p. 172).

[6] Cf. Surah 5. 50, 108.

[7] Arabic *anṣār*, plural of *naṣiru*. This is a word-play on 'Nazarenes' (*naṣārā*). The title *anṣār* was conferred after Muhammad's death on the two tribes which had supported him at Medina.

[8] Literally 'we are Muslims' (similarly in Surah 5. 111).

resurrection. Then you will all return to me and I will judge your disputes. I will inflict a severe punishment on the unbelievers in this world and the next; they will have no helpers. But those who have believed and performed the works of righteousness will receive their rewards in full. Allah does not love evil-doers.'

Thus far the signs, and the wise remembrance.

Jesus is in Allah's eyes like Adam; he created him of dust and said to him 'Be!' — and he was.

This account of the birth of Christ is chiefly based on the first chapter of the Gospel of Luke, where the angelic annunciation of a son to Mary is preceded by the angelic promise of a son (John) to the aged priest Zechariah and his wife: Zechariah's scepticism forms a contrast to Mary's faith. But there are a few elements in the account which are derived from apocryphal Gospels. The narrative of Mary's birth and Zechariah's appointment to be her guardian resembles what we are told in the *Protevangel of James* (where her parents are called Joachim and Anna). The reference to Jesus's making clay birds and imparting life to them comes from the *Infancy Gospel of Thomas*.[9]

A summarised form of this account of Jesus's works (including the breathing of life into clay birds) appears in Surah 5. 109 f. Here Allah reminds him how he protected him against the Israelites when they refused to believe the sure signs which he brought them and said, 'This is nothing but sheer magic.'[10]

A parallel account of the birth of Jesus to that in Surah 3 is given in Surah 19 (appropriately called the Surah of Mary). Here too, in accordance with the Lukan precedent, the account (verses 16–36) follows the story of the promise of a son to Zechariah:

Tell in the Book the story of Mary: how she withdrew from her people to a place in the east, and there wove a curtain to separate herself from them. Then We sent to her Our Spirit, who took the form of a comely human being. 'May the Merciful One protect me from you,' she said. 'Leave me, if you are pious.' 'I am your Lord's messenger',

[9] For these two works see p. 86 f.
[10] Cf. p. 56.

said he, 'to give you a pure son.' 'How can I have a son?' she asked. 'No man has ever touched me, nor have I been a harlot.' 'So shall it be', said he; 'your Lord has said, "It is easy for me; We shall make him a sign to the people and a blessing from Ourselves. So it is decreed."'

Thereupon she conceived, and retired to a distant place. When she felt the birth-pangs she seized the trunk of a palm-tree, and said, 'Would that I had died ere now, alike forgetting and forgotten.' Then the child called to her from beneath, 'Do not grieve! Your Lord has placed a rivulet at your feet. Shake the trunk of the palm-tree, and it will let juicy, ripe fruit fall. Eat, drink and be of good cheer. If you see any human being, say, "I have vowed a fast to the Merciful One; I will not speak to any man today."'

Then she brought him to her people, carrying him, and they said to her, 'Sister of Aaron, this is extraordinary! Your father was not a bad man nor was your mother a harlot.' So she pointed to the child, but they said, 'How can we speak to an infant in a cradle?' The child spoke up: 'Indeed, I am Allah's servant. He has given me the Book; he has made me a prophet. He has made me blessed wherever I go; he has enjoined on me as long as I live prayer and alms-giving, and filial duty to my mother; he has made me neither arrogant nor miserable. Peace be upon me the day of my birth, the day of my death and the day of my being raised up alive!'

Such was Jesus son of Mary, the true Word concerning which they doubt. Far be it from Allah that he should beget a son! When he decrees that something shall be so, he has only to say 'Be!'—and it is.

While the framework of this account is derived from Luke's nativity narrative, several of the incidents included in it exhibit an affinity to tales told in the apocryphal Infancy Gospels. The story of Mary's weaving a curtain is told in the *Protevangel of James*, where Mary is one of seven virgins of the family of David chosen to make a curtain or veil for the temple in Jerusalem. The incident of the palm-tree resembles one in the *Gospel of Pseudo-Matthew* (20: 1 f.), where Mary, during the flight into Egypt, longs for the fruit of a palm-tree, and the infant Jesus, sitting in her lap, says, 'Bend down your branches, tree, and refresh my mother with your fruit.'[11] The general idea is not unlike that of the *Cherry Tree Carol*, in which, however, it is the unborn child who issues the command:

> Bow down then the tallest tree
> For my mother to have some.

As for the insistence (repeated elsewhere in the Qur'ān)[12] that Allah has no son, this is obviously a denial of the Christian ascription to Jesus of the title 'Son of God', and equally obviously it springs from a misinterpretation of the title in a biological sense. The Christian belief in the divinity of Christ is also denied, together with the doctrine of the Trinity. Thus in Surah 5 we read (verses 76–79):

> Unbelievers are those who say, 'Allah is the Messiah, the son of Mary.'[13] On the contrary, the Messiah himself said, 'Children of Israel, serve Allah, my Lord and your Lord.' Whosoever associates anything with Allah, Allah has made the Garden[14] inaccessible to him; for him the Fire[15] is reserved. Evildoers have no helpers. Unbelievers are those who say, 'Allah is one of three.' There is only one God. If they do not desist from such language, a painful punishment will befall them. Will they then repent towards Allah and seek his pardon? Allah is forgiving and compassionate. The Messiah, the son of Mary, is only a messenger, before whose time the other messengers[16] had passed away. His mother was a faithful woman; they both ate earthly food. See, we show them clear signs, yet they become entangled in falsehood.

The surah from which this extract is quoted is entitled 'The Table', because it includes a reminiscence of the feeding of the

---

[11] The 'rivulet' is peculiar to the Qur'ān. E. F. F. Bishop suggests that it might be a reminiscence of Pilate's aqueduct, traces of which can still be seen near Bethlehem ('Is Pontius Pilate's Aqueduct referred to in the Qur'ān?' *The Muslim World* 52, 1962, pp. 189 ff.).

[12] E.g. Surah 2. 110 f.; 17. 111; 39. 6.

[13] Almost identical wording appears in Surah 5. 19.

[14] Paradise.

[15] Gehenna.

[16] The 'other messengers' are the Hebrew prophets.

multitude, or possibly of the institution of the Lord's Supper (verses 112–15):

> When the apostles said, 'Jesus son of Mary, is your Lord able to send us down a table from heaven?'[17] he replied: 'Show piety towards Allah, if you are believers.' They said, 'We desire to eat from it, that our hearts may be at peace and we may know that what you have told us is true, so that we may bear witness to it.' Then Jesus son of Mary said, 'Allah, our Lord, send us down a table from heaven, to provide a festival for us and for all who will ever come after us. Let it be a sign from you. Give us our sustenance, for you are the best of givers.'

This is followed immediately by a passage in which Jesus is represented as repudiating the later doctrine and worship of some of his followers (verses 116 f.):

> Allah said, 'Jesus son of Mary, was it you who said to the people, "Take me and my mother as two gods apart from Allah"?' He replied: 'Yours be the glory! Far be it from me to say what I have no right to say! . . . I said nothing to them but what you commanded me to say: "Serve Allah, my Lord and your Lord."'

In the comprehensive Surah 4, entitled 'Women', there are one or two crucially important paragraphs about Jesus. Of 'the people of the Book' (the Jews) we read (verses 155–7):

> They refused the truth and uttered a great slander against Mary. They said, 'We killed the Messiah, Jesus son of Mary, the messenger of Allah.' But they did not kill him, they did not crucify him; it only seemed to them to be so. Those who have disagreed about him are in doubt concerning him; they have no certain knowledge and follow only conjecture. In fact, Allah raised him to himself: Allah is sublime and wise. Everyone among the people of the Book will believe in him before his death, and on the day of resurrection he will witness against them.

[17] Cf. Psalm 78. 19 ('Can God spread a table in the wilderness?').

Then, of another 'people of the Book' (the Christians) we read later in the same *surah* (verses 169 f.):

> O people of the Book, do not go beyond due limits in your religion. Do not say anything but the truth about Allah. The Messiah, Jesus the son of Mary, was no more than Allah's messenger and his Word, which he sent forth into Mary, a spirit proceeding from him. So believe in Allah and his messengers, and do not say, 'Three.' Refrain, and it will be better for you. Allah is but one God; far be it from him to have a son! All that is in heaven and on earth is his. Let it suffice that Allah undertakes one's case. The Messiah does not disdain to be a servant of Allah, any more than the angels who are in his immediate presence.

For Muhammad and his followers Jesus is one of the greatest of men, a prophet and messenger from God in the succession of Abraham and Moses. Although he is acknowledged as the virgin-born son of Mary and described as a spirit proceeding from God, he is man and no more. If he is refused the title 'Son of God' (which was misunderstood, as we have seen, in a biological sense), he is freely admitted to be God's 'Word'[18] (which, for the fourth Evangelist, is another way of saying what is meant by the 'Son of God').

The 'slander against Mary' of which the Jews are accused is probably a tale about Jesus's birth, known to have been in circulation in the later part of the second century, which cast doubts on his legitimacy and on Mary's chastity.[19] But when they are further accused of claiming to have killed Jesus, we may wonder if Jews actually made such a claim, since historically his crucifixion was carried out by Roman executioners in

[18] But the designation 'Word' in this context has not the same sense for Muhammad as for John; for Muhammad it may have meant a bearer of the Word, a messenger. E. F. F. Bishop recalls how, in preparation for a tense weekend about 1920, a Cairo daily newspaper 'printed a prayer to be used the ensuing Friday, Saturday and Sunday, in mosque, synagogue and church — offered in the names of Muhammad the Apostle of God, Jesus the Word of God and Moses who fled from slavery' ('Syncretism and Monotheistic Faith', *Anglican Theological Review* 42, 1960, p. 202).
[19] According to Origen (*Against Celsus* i. 32), Celsus in his *True Discourse* (c. A.D. 170) introduced a Jew who maintained that Mary bore Jesus to a soldier named Pantheras (a name which, if it is a corruption of Greek *parthenos*, 'virgin', could be an unintentional testimony to the belief in Jesus's virginal conception). See pp. 57 f.

accordance with the sentence of a Roman court. We might ask if Muhammad is not here taking over a Christian charge against the Jews—but he may, on the other hand, be dependent on an account similar to that quoted above from the *baraitha* in the tractate *Sanhedrin*, which implies that the death sentence was passed on Jesus by a Jewish court for an offence against Jewish religious law.[20]

In one or two passages quoted above from the Qur'ān there are vague references to the 'death' of Jesus,[21] but this passage in Surah 4 emphatically denies his death, or at least the accepted account of it. 'They did not kill him, they did not crucify him; it only seemed to them to be so'—or 'it was made a semblance to them'. The explanation of this in Muslim tradition is that someone else, with the appearance of Jesus, was crucified, while Jesus himself was caught up into heaven. This may very well be what the Qur'ān intends.

But, if so, we are faced with a paradoxical situation. For all his insistence on the real humanity of Jesus, Muhammad seems to have derived his view of the crucifixion from a source which denied Jesus's real humanity, and therewith the genuineness of his death. This denial belongs to the doctrine which was called Docetism because it maintained that Jesus only *seemed* to have a real human nature and to die a real death. Against an early form of this doctrine John the Evangelist contended both in his Gospel and in his Letters.[22] The Docetists interpreted the crucifixion narrative in several different ways, but one way was by suggesting that someone else (Simon of Cyrene, according to some)[23] was mistaken for Jesus and crucified in his place. That Jesus was *not* crucified has thus become practically a dogma in Islam.[24] A corollary of this dogma is that the

---

[20] See p. 56.

[21] Surah 3. 48 (p. 170); 19. 34 (p. 172).

[22] Cf. John 1. 14; 19. 34 f.; 1 John 4. 2; 5. 6. See also above, p. 93.

[23] Irenaeus (*Against Heresies* i. 24. 2) ascribes this idea to Basilides, but this conflicts with the words of Basilides quoted by Clement of Alexandria (*Miscellanies* iv. 12), to the effect that Christ suffered like any other martyr. See p. 178.

[24] W. M. Watt, however, thinks it might be understood in a sense not unlike that of John 10. 17 f., where Jesus says: 'I lay down my life, that I may take it again. No one takes it from me, but I lay it down of my own accord' (*Islamic Revelation in the Modern World* [Edinburgh U.P., 1969], pp. 54 ff.).

testimonies to his crucifixion in the Christian Gospels must be corruptions.

The Syrian Christianity from which Muhammad derived his knowledge of the story of Jesus is also responsible for his understanding of the doctrine of the Trinity. No doubt it appeared to him as a belief in three deities, which flatly contradicted the monotheistic principle, but it appears further that he understood these three to be Jesus and his mother in addition to God the Father. This, of course, is far from the orthodox trinitarianism of the Nicene Creed and similar formularies. But in the Semitic languages the word for 'spirit' is feminine, and we have already seen evidence of a tendency to equate the Spirit with the mother of Jesus.[25]

While it is interesting to try to trace the sources from which the references to Jesus and Christian beginnings in the Qur'ān were derived, we do not in the nature of the case find any fresh information about him there.

[25] See p. 101.

Chapter Ten

Jesus in Islamic Tradition

THE Qur'ān is not the only work of Muslim literature to contain statements about the deeds and words of Jesus, although it is, of course, the norm for pious Muslims in this as in all other respects. Islamic tradition has a good deal to say about him, but its lateness diminishes its value, except where it appears to have drawn upon much earlier sources.

One of the leading transmitters of Jewish and Christian teaching to his fellow-Muslims was Wahb ben Munabbih, who lived around A.D. 700. He transmitted an outline of the passion narrative which followed the New Testament account fairly closely, except that he brought it into line with the Qur'ān by stating that Jesus's enemies did not put him to death on the cross.

> They brought him to the gibbet on which they intended to crucify him, but God raised him up to himself and a simulacrum was crucified in his place. He remained there for seven hours, and then his mother and another woman whom he had cured of madness[1] came to weep for him. But Jesus came to them and said: 'God has raised me up to himself,[2] and this is merely a simulacrum.'

This is the form in which Wahb's outline was reproduced by al-Tabarī, an historian and commentator on the Qur'ān, in the second half of the ninth century. But over a century later (*c.* 1000) another writer, al-Tha'labī, amplified this outline by affirming that Jesus's place on the cross was taken by no mere simulacrum or phantom, but by another man.[3] (The rather vague

---

[1] Plainly a reference to Mary Magdalene (cf. Luke 8. 2; Matthew 28. 1).
[2] See p. 174.
[3] Here the other man is Judas Iscariot; a much earlier (second-century) suggestion was that he was Simon of Cyrene (see p. 176 with n. 23).

statement in the Qur'ān could be interpreted in either of these ways.)[4] When Jesus was brought to the cross —

darkness covered the earth, and God sent angels who took up their position between them [the executioners] and Jesus. The shape of Jesus was put upon Judas who had pointed him out, and they crucified him instead, supposing that he was Jesus. After three hours God took Jesus to himself and raised him up to heaven . . .

One of the most important Muslim writers on this subject is 'Abd al-Jabbār, chief *kadi* (judge) of the city of Rayy (modern Teheran). In A.D. 995 'Abd al-Jabbār wrote an Arabic treatise in order to vindicate Muhammad's claim to be a true prophet. Since the Christians were foremost among those who denied this claim, 'Abd al-Jabbār devoted a substantial section of his treatise to their arguments,[5] and carried the war into the enemy camp by charging the Christians with doctrinal inconsistency and with corrupting Jesus's original teaching. His information about Christian beliefs and practices appears to have been derived from ex-Christians who had been converted to Islam. There are many references to the New Testament writings, but 'Abd al-Jabbār was specially interested in some accounts of Jesus, stemming ultimately from uncanonical sources, which seemed to him to confirm Muhammad's statements. Some of these sources were Jewish-Christian records, with which 'Abd al-Jabbār agreed in so far as they portrayed Jesus as a pious and observant son of Abraham who made no divine claims for himself, although he disagreed with them when, for example, they denied his virgin birth.[6] He refers to one Gospel which began: 'This is the generation of Jesus the

---

[4] See p. 176.

[5] On this section see the important studies by S. M. Stern, 'Quotations from Apocryphal Gospels in 'Abd al-Jabbār', *Journal of Theological Studies*, new series 18 (1967), pp. 34 ff., and "'Abd al-Jabbār's Account of how Christ's Religion was Falsified by the Adoption of Roman Customs', *Journal of Theological Studies*, new series 19 (1968), pp. 128 ff.

[6] Compare another incident quoted by 'Abd al-Jabbār as coming from the Christians' 'gospels and stories': 'When he was crucified, his mother Mary came with her children, James, Simon and Judah, and stood before him. He said to her from the gibbet: "Take your children and begone!"' (For James, Simon and Judah cf. Matthew 13. 35; Mark 6. 3.)

son of Joseph the carpenter.' This could well have been an Ebionite edition of the Gospel of Matthew; the Ebionites are said to have regarded Jesus as a man born of human parents who for his righteousness was 'adopted' by God as his Son.[7]

One passion narrative which 'Abd al-Jabbār quotes says that Pilate, 'king of the Romans', arrested Jesus and handed him over to the Jews, who had lodged a complaint against him.

> They put him on a donkey, facing backwards, placed a crown of thorns on his head and led him around to expose him to public ridicule. They struck him from behind and then came round to his face and said, 'King of Israel, who did that to you?' Then he became weary and exhausted, and asked for a drink of water to quench his thirst. They took a bitter herb and squeezed it out, put vinegar into it and gave it to him.[8] He took it, thinking that it was water, but, when he tasted how bitter it was, he spat it out. But they poured it down his nose and kept on ill-treating him all day and night. Next morning, which was Passion Friday (as they call it) they asked Pilate to scourge him, and he did so. Then they took him and crucified him, and pierced him with lances. While he was on the gibbet he kept on crying, 'My God, why have you forsaken me? My God, why have you forgotten me?'—until he died. Then he was taken down from the cross and buried.

'Abd al-Jabbār, of course, did not accept this account; it contradicted the Qur'ān, according to which Jesus was not really crucified. This, he says, is the story as it is told by Christians and Jews (by Jews, at least, in so far as they agreed that Jesus was actually put to death). But he himself regarded as more satisfactory another account which also came from a Christian source.

According to this account Pilate, 'king of the Romans', had an adjutant named Herod. Herod was approached on Thursday

---

[7] The Ebionites are first credited with this opinion by Irenaeus (*Heresies* i. 26. 2); but it is probably they who are referred to by Justin when he speaks of some who 'acknowledge Jesus to be Christ while declaring that he was man sprung from men' (*Dialogue with Trypho* 48. 4). See p. 105.

[8] Based on Psalm 69. 21: 'They gave me gall for food, and for my thirst they gave me vinegar to drink' (see p. 89).

of Passover week by 'the Jews', who reported that Jesus corrupted and misled their youth. Herod ordered that Jesus should be arrested and brought before him. The arrest was facilitated by Judas Iscariot, who undertook for thirty silver coins to point Jesus out to 'the Jews' and Herod's guards by kissing him. But Judas, out of friendship for Jesus, kissed another man in the crowd of pilgrims, and this unfortunate man was brought before Herod. He was so panic-stricken that he could not speak, except that when he was charged with claiming to be the Messiah he stammered out: 'It is they who say so; not I.' Herod began to suspect that it was a trumped-up charge and, calling for a ewer of water, washed his hands and sent the man to Pilate. Pilate similarly found no substance in the charge. But instead of being released, the man was locked up overnight, and then follows the story of his mockery, ill-treatment, scourging and crucifixion on the lines of the passion narrative which 'Abd al-Jabbār has already quoted.[9] But there is a new sequel:

Judas met the Jews and said to them: 'What have you done with the man whom you took into custody yesterday?' 'We have crucified him,' said they. Judas was appalled, but they assured him that they had really done so, adding: 'If you want to know for certain, go to that field of melons.'[10] He went, and when he saw him he said: 'This is innocent blood; this is guiltless blood.' Then, cursing the Jews, he took the thirty silver coins which they had given him as payment for his betrayal and flung them in their faces, after which he went home and hanged himself.[11]

This account bears some resemblance to the docetic *Gospel of Peter*,[12] but whereas that work makes Pilate wash his hands and leave the dirty work to Herod, now Herod (transformed into an adjutant of Pilate 'king of the Romans') is also exonerated, and the dirty work is left to 'the Jews', who, deceived by Judas, crucify an unknown and innocent man in place of Jesus.

[9] See p. 180 (the narrative is reproduced as far as the words 'until he died').
[10] The field of melons is perhaps based on the 'garden' of John 19. 41.
[11] Cf. Matthew 27. 3–5.
[12] See pp. 88 ff.

For all its defects, this account commended itself to 'Abd al-Jabbār because here, he thought, was a *Christian* source confirming Muhammad's statement that Jesus was not crucified. 'Christian' after a fashion the source may have been, but its docetic tendency and its flight from history stamp it as something which could be approved only by one who, like 'Abd al-Jabbār, was dogmatically predisposed to approve it.

'Abd al-Jabbār's section on the Christians has been brought into the limelight in recent years because of a claim that it depends in some degree on a Jewish or Jewish-Christian document which deserves to be recognised as a reasonably early and respectable version of the origins of Christianity.[13] According to this version, it was Paul who first transformed Jesus into a divine being and an object of worship. But our confidence in what it says about Paul is shaken when we find that Paul was sent by the Roman governor of Judaea to *Constantinople*, where he won the good will of the empress. So radically did he corrupt the teaching of Jesus that, instead of turning the Romans into Christians, he turned the Christians into Romans: the features which distinguish Christians from Jews and Muslims are features taken over from Roman paganism (including, forsooth, the law that men may not divorce their wives). Nemesis caught up with Paul when he was crucified — horizontally![14] — by Nero, an emperor who flourished shortly *after* Titus[15] (the destroyer of Jerusalem) and shortly before Constantine.

We have already mentioned an alleged saying of Jesus — 'This world is a bridge . . .' — which was preserved in Islamic tradition.[16] There is, in fact, a wealth of sayings attributed to Jesus in Islamic tradition, but they are mostly quoted in later works by ascetic writers of the eleventh and twelfth centuries.

---

[13] This claim was published by S. Pines in 'The Jewish Christians of the Early Centuries of Christianity according to a New Source', *Proceedings of the Israel Academy of Sciences and Humanities* ii. 13 (Jerusalem, 1966). It was earlier reported in more popular form, e.g. in *Time*, July 15, 1966, p. 64.

[14] At his own request, because he said he was not worthy to be crucified vertically, as Jesus was. A similar story was told in the mid-second century about Peter, who chose to be crucified head downwards (*Acts of Peter* 37 f.; Eusebius, *Hist. Eccl.* iii. 1. 2, perhaps on Origen's authority).

[15] Nero was emperor A.D. 54–68; Titus, A.D. 79–81; Constantine, A.D. 306–37. According to the story told by 'Abd al-Jabbār, Titus was well-disposed to Paul, but Nero later exposed him as an impostor.

[16] See p. 130.

A few go back to the earliest decades of Islam, in the seventh century. They are too late to receive serious consideration as genuine utterances of Jesus, except where their derivation from much earlier sources can be established. The fullest collection of these sayings was brought together by a Spanish scholar, M. Asin y Palacios, in two numbers of *Patrologia Orientalis* (Paris), vol. 13, no. 3 (1916), and vol. 19, no. 4 (1926). There 233 sayings are reproduced in Arabic, with a Latin translation and commentary.[17] A dozen will serve as samples:

1. Jesus (whom God preserve) said: 'How many trees there are! But they do not all bear fruit. How many kinds of fruit there are! But they are not all good. How many forms of knowledge there are! But they are not all profitable.'[18]

The figure of trees and fruit appears in a few places in the Gospels (e.g. Matthew 7. 16–20; Luke 13. 6–9; John 15. 1–6).

2. Jesus (whom God preserve) said: 'Do not hang pearls on the necks of pigs, for wisdom is better than pearls, and whoso despises it is worse than pigs.'[19]

This is reminiscent of the warning not to cast pearls before swine (Matthew 7. 6), but the reference to wisdom reminds us of the proverb about 'a gold ring in a swine's snout' (Proverbs 11. 22); cf. Proverbs 3. 15: 'she [wisdom] is more precious than jewels'.

3. Jesus (whom God preserve) said: 'How shall he be reckoned among the wise who, having set his feet on the way to the life to come, turns his steps back towards the way of this world? And how shall he be reckoned among the wise who seeks the Word in order to preach it to others and not to fulfil it in practice?'[20]

---

[17] There is a smaller collection of 77 sayings by D. S. Margoliouth in a series of articles entitled 'Christ in Islam' in *The Expository Times* 5 (1893–1894), pp. 59, 107, 177 f., 503 f., 561. Cf. also R. Dunkerley, 'The Muhammadan Agrapha', *The Expository Times* 39 (1927–28), pp. 167 ff., 230 ff.

[18] Al-Ghazzali, *Revival of the Religious Sciences* i. 24. 5.

[19] Al-Ghazzali, *Revival* i. 43. 4.

[20] Al-Ghazzali, *Revival* i. 46. 14.

The first part of this saying resembles the warning that one who puts his hand to the plough and turns back is unfit for the kingdom of God (Luke 9. 62). The second part may have some contact with Jesus's insistence on the importance of doing what he says as well as merely hearing it (Matthew 7. 24–27; Luke 6. 46–49), or his criticism of those scribes who 'preach, but do not practise' (Matthew 23. 2 f.); cf. 1 Corinthians 9. 27; James 1. 22.

4. Jesus (whom God preserve) said: 'Blessed is he who relinquishes present desire for an absent promise which he has not yet seen.'[21]

The thought is that of renouncing temporal and material goods for the sake of eternal life (cf. Luke 18. 29 f.), of walking by faith and not by sight (cf. 2 Corinthians 5. 7; Hebrews 11. 1).

5. Jesus (whom God preserve) said: 'The love of this world and of the life to come cannot co-exist in the believer's heart, any more than water and fire can co-exist in the same vessel.'[22]

This is to the same effect as Jesus's insistence on the impossibility of serving God and mammon[23] (Matthew 6. 24; Luke 16. 13); cf. John 12. 25; James 4. 4; 1 John 2. 15–17.

6. Jesus (whom God preserve) said: 'He who seeks the world is like a man who drinks sea-water: the more he drinks, the more thirsty he becomes, until at last it kills him.'[24]

This inculcates the same lesson as the preceding saying; cf. also John 4. 13: 'Every one who drinks of this water will thirst again' (although that was fresh water, not salt).

7. The Messiah (whom God preserve) said: 'Blessed is he to whom God has taught his book, but let him not thereafter die in pride.'[25]

[21] Al-Ghazzali, *Revival* iii. 48. 8.
[22] Al-Ghazzali, *Revival* iii. 140. 10.
[23] See p. 131.
[24] Al-Ghazzali, *Revival* iii. 149. 5.
[25] Al-Ghazzali, *Revival* iii. 235. 21.

Cf. 1 Corinthians 4. 7: 'What have you that you did not receive? If then you received it, why do you boast as if it were not a gift?' Cf. also Romans 2. 17 ff.

8. The Messiah (whom God bless and preserve) said to the children of Israel: 'I recommend to you pure water, woodland herbs and barley bread. But avoid wheaten bread, for you will never be able to give God adequate thanks for it!'[26]

Where barley was the staple food of the common people (cf. the 'five barley loaves' of John 6. 9), wheat was reckoned a luxury, reserved for rich folk.

9. It is related of Jesus the son of Mary (may God abundantly bless them both and preserve them!) that he said: 'O assembly of wise men! You have left the way of truth and loved the world. Nevertheless, as kings have left wisdom to you, so do you leave worldly dominion to them.'[27]

The last clause might have a remote contact with Mark 12. 17: 'Render to Caesar the things that are Caesar's.'[28]

10. It is related that Jesus (whom God preserve) said to his apostles: 'I have not taught you in order that you should be proud; I have taught you in order that you should work. Wisdom is not the utterance of wisdom but the practice of wisdom.'[29]

Like Saying 3, this emphasises the necessity of practising and not merely preaching.

11. Jesus (whom God preserve) said: 'I have two friends. He who loves them loves me; he who hates them, hates me. They are poverty and the mortification of greed.'[30]

This may be a vivid recasting of such Gospel sayings as

[26] Al-Ghazzali, *Revival* iv. 164. 14.
[27] Samarqandi, *Awakening of the Negligent* 190. 12.
[28] See pp. 149, 162.
[29] Ibn 'Abd al-Barr, *Breviary* 100. 8.
[30] Al-Ghazzali, *Epitome of the Revival of the Religious Sciences* 246. 16.

'How hárd it will be for those who have riches to enter the kingdom of God!' (Mark 10. 23) and 'Take heed, and beware of all covetousness' (Luke 12. 15).

12. The Messiah (whom God preserve) said: 'O assembly of apostles! How many lamps are blown out by the wind! How many servants of God are corrupted by vanity!'[31]

In short, only those who endure to the end attain salvation (Mark 13. 13).

These are but a few out of many more sayings attributed to Jesus in Islamic tradition; the medieval date of so many of them probably reflects the impact made by Syriac Christianity in its eastward advance during those centuries.[32]

---

[31] Al-Ghazzali, *Epitome* 63. 14.

[32] Cf. K. S. Latourette, *A History of the Expansion of Christianity* ii (New York, 1938; reprinted Paternoster Press, Exeter, 1971), pp. 263 ff.

Chapter Eleven

The Evidence of Archaeology

DIRECT contemporary archaeological evidence of Jesus and his immediate followers should no more be expected than contemporary literary evidence. It is only in exceptional circumstances that people not judged important in their lifetime have their names archaeologically attested. True, Sir Mortimer Wheeler quotes 'a classic sentence' to the effect that 'a great nation may leave behind it a very poor rubbish-heap'. But the archaeologist is interested in bigger and better rubbish-heaps, because from them he can reconstruct the social life and culture of the people who left them as their memorials. 'And are we, as practising archaeologists', asks Sir Mortimer, 'to award the palm to the unknown Sumerian who was buried at Ur with sixty-three helmeted soldiers, grooms, and gold-garlanded damsels, two chariots and six bullocks, or to the Nazarene in a loin-cloth who was nailed up on Golgotha between two thieves?' He feels that, 'were archaeology alone the arbiter, the answer would not be in doubt'; but reminds us not to overlook 'the missing values that cannot be appraised in inches or soil-samples or smudges in the earth'.[1]

Paul, as he moved along the streets of Athens, could see not only the altar-inscription 'To an unknown God' but many another inscription, and not only images of the gods but statues of famous men. The visitor to Athens today can see the complete Greek text of Paul's speech of Acts 17. 22–31 inscribed on bronze at the foot of the ascent to the Areopagus ('Mars' Hill') and several statues stand in his honour in the city where he was executed. But these memorials are of more recent date; no one during Paul's lifetime or for many years after, in Athens or Rome or anywhere else, thought him worthy even of the modest type of plaque which, in many places in the United

---

[1] *Archaeology from the Earth* (Pelican Books, 1956), p. 243.

Kingdom, commemorates the fact that 'John Wesley preached here'.

We know from a contemporary bust what Nero looked like, but our idea of Paul's appearance has grown up in the course of tradition.[2] Naturally so; by all accepted standards of that day Nero, to whose judgment Paul appealed, was a much more important person than Paul. How could their contemporaries foresee a day when this estimate would be reversed — when (as someone has said) men would call their dogs Nero and their sons Paul?

It was not until a hundred years after Peter and Paul were executed in Rome under Nero that, so far as we can tell, an attempt was made by the Christians of the city to erect unpretentious monuments to mark the sites of their martyrdom, or of their burial. It was not until the fourth century that the site in Jerusalem of Jesus's crucifixion, death and resurrection was marked by the first buildings to be erected in the area now covered by the Church of the Holy Sepulchre. Jacob's well near Shechem (modern Nablus), where Jesus held his conversation with the Samaritan woman (John 4. 6), can be identified with certainty, and so can the Pools of Bethesda (John 5. 2) and Siloam (John 9. 7) in Jerusalem; but such natural features persist from century to century. The temple area in Jerusalem survives as the Haram esh-Sherif (the 'Noble Enclosure') with the Dome of the Rock covering the ancient rock of sacrifice; and indeed excavations around the perimeter of the area since 1967 have brought to light valuable evidence from the New Testament period.

Memorials and incidental references to emperors and other influential people who are mentioned in the pages of the New Testament are not lacking. But when we think in general of archaeology in relation to the New Testament, we think of very many different kinds of remains which have come down to us in the Eastern Mediterranean lands from the first century A.D.,

[2] The earliest literary description of Paul's appearance is given in the *Acts of Paul*, written *c.* A.D. 160: he is described as 'a man small in stature, with meeting eyebrows, with a rather large nose, bald-headed, bow-legged, strongly built, full of charm, for at times he looked like a man, and at times he had the face of an angel'. The last part belongs to the conventional description of saints (cf. Acts 6. 15), but the main body of the pen-portrait is so vigorous that it has sometimes been thought to depend on good oral tradition preserved in Asia Minor.

or the periods immediately preceding and following that century, especially when they throw light on the text, narrative or ideas of the New Testament. Manuscripts, coins, inscriptions, sepulchres, ossuaries, inscribed potsherds, ancient buildings, ancient cities — all these have their contribution to make to our subject.

Papyrus Documents

One collection of manuscripts (the Dead Sea Scrolls) has already been mentioned in our chapter on 'Preparation for the Messiah'. These manuscripts are mainly written on skin but partly on papyrus.

Papyrus is a rush plant whose inner bark was dried in strips; these strips were then gummed together so as to form conveniently sized sheets and rolls of writing material. People wrote on it with reed pens, and used an ink which was compounded of charcoal, gum and water.

For all its convenience as a writing material, papyrus was not at all durable; it rotted quickly when exposed to damp. So, while it was in common use in many parts of the ancient world, papyrus documents have survived only in such dry environments as the Egyptian desert, the volcanic ash of Herculaneum, and parts of the wilderness of Judaea.

In Egypt papyrus was used as a writing material from ancient days, but in connection with the New Testament we are concerned only with papyrus documents from the closing centuries B.C. and the early centuries A.D., when there was a large Greek-speaking population in and around Alexandria. This Greek-speaking population was thoroughly literate; the common people wrote letters and kept the commercial accounts of everyday life on pieces of papyrus. For odd jottings an even cheaper writing material was always available in broken pieces of unglazed earthenware, pieces which are known by the Greek term *ostraca*.

When these papyrus scraps and fragments of pottery had served their immediate purpose, they were thrown out on to the rubbish heap, and lay there forgotten and undisturbed for centuries. But towards the end of last century some of them were discovered and soon became an object of interest to New Testament scholars. Many papyri containing literary texts have also been found, but more interesting from the standpoint of New Testament studies were the unliterary fragments on which could be traced what ordinary people wrote in their common vernacular. The reason was that this common vernacular turned out to be remarkably similar to the Greek in which much of the New Testament (especially the narrative parts) is written.

Our great biblical scholars, trained in the classical Greek of the fifth century B.C., had for long recognised the differences between it and the Greek in which the New Testament was written. But they were not sure how to account for these differences. One German scholar, writing in 1863, could describe New Testament Greek as 'a language of the Holy Ghost',[3] with the implication that it was a special form of Greek divinely invented for the purpose. But in that very year Joseph Barber Lightfoot (later Bishop of Durham), lecturing in Cambridge, expressed his conviction 'that if we could only recover letters that ordinary people wrote to each other, without any thought of being literary, we should have the greatest possible help for the understanding of the New Testament'.[4]

Lightfoot could not have known how soon his words would be confirmed by actual discoveries. For when, a few years later, the attention of New Testament students was attracted to the vernacular papyrus fragments from Egypt, it turned out that the 'language of the Holy Ghost' was largely identical with the language of the common people—a fact which has certain practical lessons for writers and preachers to take to heart.

The pioneer in the study of the Greek vernacular papyri and their application to New Testament studies was a German scholar, Adolf Deissmann;[5] among British scholars who made notable contributions to the same study two pre-eminent names are those of James Hope Moulton, Professor in Manchester, and George Milligan, Professor in Glasgow.[6] Like all new discoveries, this one had excessive claims made on its behalf to begin with.

[3] Richard Rothe, *Zur Dogmatik* (Gotha, 1863), p. 238.

[4] As quoted by J. H. Moulton, *A Grammar of New Testament Greek: Prolegomena* (Edinburgh, 1906), p. 242.

[5] Deissmann's best-known work on this subject is his *Light from the Ancient East* (London, 1927).

[6] Editors of *The Vocabulary of the Greek Testament* (Edinburgh, 1930).

There are parts of the New Testament where we find more linguistic help in Greek literature, or in the Septuagint (the pre-Christian Greek translation of the Old Testament); but it remains true that over wide areas of the book the vernacular papyri have thrown new and welcome light.

To give but one example: the Greek word *epiousios*, translated 'daily' in the petition 'Give us this day our daily bread', had long been debated by theologians and philologists. Some had given it a mystical meaning, as when the Douai Bible, following Jerome, speaks of 'supersubstantial bread'; others put a more mundane construction on it, as when James Moffatt rendered the petition, 'give us to-day our bread for the morrow'. The adjective *epiousios* was unknown elsewhere in Greek literature, and it was this that caused the uncertainty about its meaning. But when in 1889 it was identified in a papyrus document in a context which showed that the meaning was 'daily rations', this was generally recognised as fixing its meaning in the Lord's Prayer. (Unfortunately the document was subsequently lost, so the reading can no longer be checked.)[7]

Sometimes a scrap of papyrus will throw incidental light on a custom alluded to in passing by a New Testament writer. Paul, for example, in 1 Corinthians 8. 10, envisages the situation in which a Christian might be seen 'at table in an idol's temple', and later he warns such a person that he 'cannot partake of the table of the Lord and the table of demons' (10. 21). That the devotee of a pagan deity might invite his friends to a banquet in that deity's temple is illustrated by a few letters of invitation found among the Oxyrhynchus papyri, after this fashion:

Chaeremon invites you to dine at the table of the Lord Sarapis in the Sarapeion tomorrow, the 15th, at the 9th hour.[8]

The Sarapeion was the temple of Sarapis, a deity much venerated in Egypt in Graeco-Roman times. If we have no samples of comparable invitations from Corinth, that is

[7] Cf. B. M. Metzger, 'How many times does *epiousios* occur outside the Lord's Prayer?' *Expository Times* 69 (1957–58), pp. 52 ff., reprinted in his *Historical and Literary Studies* (Leiden, 1968), pp. 64 ff.

[8] P. Oxy. 110; cf. 523, 1484, 1755.

because Corinth does not provide the environmental situation in which such unconsidered trifles could be preserved intact throughout the centuries. Some further papyrus documents will be mentioned in other contexts.

Census-taking in Judaea

Much debate has been occasioned over many years by the statement in Luke 2. 1 that, just before the birth of Jesus — elsewhere said to have occurred while Herod was still king of the Jews (i.e. before March, 4 B.C.) — 'a decree went out from Caesar Augustus that all the world should be enrolled'. By 'all the world' we are plainly to understand the Roman Empire. Three questions in particular are raised by Luke's account. (1) Could such a census have been held by the Roman Emperor in Judaea at a time when Herod ruled that territory as a nominally independent king, 'friend and ally of the Roman people'? (2) Is there evidence of such an empire-wide enrolment at that time? (3) Would such a census have involved the return of every householder to his original home, as Luke implies?

Sometimes a fourth question is asked: Was Quirinius governor of Syria at that time? Probably not. We know that he was sent by Augustus as governor (imperial legate) of Syria in A.D. 6, and it may well be that he had held a similar appointment before, but not necessarily in Syria.[9] The question, however, is based on the common translation of Luke 2. 2: 'This was the first enrolment, when Quirinius was governor of Syria.' But if we adopt the equally permissible translation, 'This enrolment (census) was before that made when Quirinius was governor of Syria', no difficulty arises in this regard. Quirinius's arrival as governor of Syria coincided with the reconstitution of Judaea as a province of the Roman Empire. (For over forty years it had been ruled by King Herod and, after him, by his son Archelaus.)[10] Now that Judaea was a Roman province, it had to pay tribute annually to the emperor, so a census was held under the supervision of Quirinius to assess the amount of tribute which the new province should be

---

[9] This is based on an imperfect Latin inscription, the *Titulus Tiburtinus* (CIL xiv. 3613), recording the career of a Roman official whose name has been lost but who is usually, but not universally, supposed to have been Quirinius.

[10] Cf. Matthew 2. 22.

required to pay. This was the occasion when, in the words of Acts 5. 37, 'Judas the Galilaean arose in the days of the census and drew away some of the people after him', teaching them that it was sacrilegious for Israelites thus to acknowledge the sovereignty of a pagan monarch over the Holy Land.[11] Although his rising was crushed, the issue which he raised remained a live one for decades, as is evident from the incident recorded in Mark 12. 13–17, where Jesus is asked if it is lawful to pay tribute to Caesar or not.[12]

According to a Latin inscription, the *Titulus Venetus*,[13] set up at Beirut by one of Quirinius's officers, the census in Judaea was held in the context of a more widespread census held in the province of Syria—apparently part of a census held throughout the Roman provinces at intervals of fourteen years from the principate of Augustus until at least the third century A.D., the present one being dated in A.D. 5–6. Proclamations and returns in connection with these recurring censuses are particularly well attested in Egypt, because of the climatic conditions under which papyri were preserved there much better than elsewhere in the Roman Empire.[14]

We come then to our three questions and answer them one by one.

(1) There are explicit statements in Josephus that towards the end of Herod's reign over Judaea (37–4 B.C.) the Emperor Augustus treated him as a subject rather than 'friend and ally', and we know that all Judaea was obliged to take an oath of allegiance to Augustus and Herod.[15] That an imperial census might be imposed on a 'client kingdom' such as Judaea was at that time is confirmed by the instance of the imposition of such a census on the 'client kingdom' of Archelaus II in Cappadocia, Eastern Asia Minor, when Tiberius was emperor (A.D. 36).[16]

(2) If such a census was held in Judaea in Herod's reign, it could have been the regular census imposed on the provinces in 10–9 B.C. (possibly the first of the fourteen-yearly series),

[11] Josephus, *War* ii. 433; *Antiquities* xvii. 355, xviii. 1 ff.
[12] See pp. 149, 162.
[13] CIL iii. 6687.
[14] I have discussed this subject at greater length in a chapter, 'Census Papyri', in *Documents of New Testament Times*, ed. A. R. Millard (London, forthcoming).
[15] Josephus, *Antiquities* xvii. 42.
[16] Tacitus, *Annals* vi. 41.

deferred for two or three years because of the special status of Judaea. There are scattered pieces of evidence for census-taking in various parts of the Empire in 10–9 B.C. and immediately after, the evidence from Egypt being practically conclusive.

(3) There is explicit evidence that the practice of requiring each householder to return to his original home for census purposes was enforced in Egypt. A papyrus document of A.D. 104 has preserved a decree of the prefect of Egypt embodying just such a direction for householders in his province.[17] Once again, the evidence comes from Egypt because such evidence is most easily preserved in Egypt, but the practice need not have been confined to Egypt.

Coins

Coins, providing a much more durable record than papyrus documents, have come down to us in great quantities from New Testament times. The Roman Emperors made plentiful use of the imperial coinage for propaganda purposes. A whole series of coins records Roman dealings with Judaea, from Pompey's occupation of the province in 63 B.C. to the suppression of the Jewish rebellion by Titus in A.D. 70, and on beyond that to Hadrian's suppression of the second Jewish rebellion in A.D. 135. 'Judaea Captured' (A.D. 70); 'The Calumny of the Jewish Tax Removed' (A.D. 96)—these and similar legends on coins bear witness to a military exploit or a piece of imperial policy.

The silver denarius exhibiting on the obverse Tiberius's name and likeness—the coin which was produced at Jesus's request in connection with the question about the tribute-money[18]—is common enough and can be bought at a reasonable price from the right kind of antiquarian. The goddess Peace sits enthroned on the reverse side, together with the title *Pontifex Maximus*.

Sometimes a point of New Testament chronology can be cleared up by reference to a coin. What was the year when Felix was replaced as procurator of Judaea by Porcius Festus (Acts 24. 27)? Our authorities vary between A.D. 55 and 60. Yet if

[17] P. Lond. 904.
[18] Mark 12. 15 f. (see p. 149).

we could be sure of the year, we should have an important criterion for establishing the chronology of Paul's career around this time. A new Judaean coinage was introduced in Nero's fifth year, before October of A.D. 59, and the most reasonable account of the introduction of this new coinage is that it marks a change in procuratorship—the change, that is to say, from Felix to Festus. If this surmise is right, then those chronologers are probably correct who bring Paul from Greece and Macedonia to Jerusalem in A.D. 57 and make him arrive in Rome from Judaea in A.D. 60.

Stone Inscriptions

One very important piece of archaeological evidence for the chronology of Paul's ministry is provided by an inscription not on a coin but on a monument of limestone. This monument, at Delphi, in Central Greece, records an edict of the Emperor Claudius,[19] and is to be dated in the first seven months of A.D. 52. Its relevance to the New Testament is that it refers to Gallio as proconsul of Achaia. Now, Luke tells us that Gallio became proconsul of Achaia during Paul's ministry of eighteen months in Corinth, the chief city of that province (Acts 18. 11 ff.). Gallio, we know from other (literary) sources,[20] governed Achaia for a short time only; he had to relinquish it because of ill health. Since proconsuls entered on their term of office on July 1 the inscription at Delphi leads us to conclude that he became proconsul on July 1, A.D. 51.[21] Since Paul's period of ministry in Corinth came to an end just in time to let him reach Jerusalem for a festival which is probably to be identified with Passover[22] we may not be far wrong in supposing that it lasted from the late summer of A.D. 50 to the early spring of A.D. 52. This piece of archaeological evidence thus provides us with a fixed point in Paul's career from which we can plot the chronology of his movements both before and after.

Another imperial decree, probably issued by the same emperor, is recorded on a slab of white marble in the Cabinet des

[19] The inscription is given in W. Dittenberger's *Sylloge Inscriptionum Graecarum* ii³, 801.

[20] From his brother Seneca's *Epistulae Morales* 104. 1.

[21] Or, just possibly (but less probably) twelve months later.

[22] In the Western text of Acts 18. 21 Paul says, 'I must without fail keep the coming festival in Jerusalem'.

Médailles in Paris.[23] So far as can be gathered, this slab came from Nazareth; it contains a severe warning against disturbing sepulchres. The situation behind this decree has been reconstructed by some scholars as follows. In the reign of Claudius (A.D. 41–54) Christianity was spreading through the Gentile world, and was coming increasingly to the notice of the custodians of law and order. The narrative of Acts offers sufficient testimony to the riots that were apt to be stirred up when Christianity came to a place for the first time, especially if there was a Jewish community in the place. The Emperor Claudius had the kind of mind which is interested in tracing things back to their origins, and if he found that Christianity, the occasion of so much public unrest, could be traced back to 'one Jesus, who was dead, whom his followers affirmed to be alive'[24] because his tomb had been found empty, he might well have decided to check any repetition of such trouble by setting up stern prohibitions of interference with tombs at various places which were associated with the rise of Christianity, as was Nazareth.

Troubles under Claudius

The unrest which affected many Jewish communities throughout the Roman Empire is reflected in the accusation brought against Paul and his friends before the civic authorities in Thessalonica (Acts 17. 6). The wording of the accusation in the Authorized Version is so well-worn as to have become quite smooth: 'These that have turned the world upside down are come hither also.' There is nothing sinister in this to ears that have been long attuned to it; it has even been taken as a text in church by preachers – more particularly, youthful preachers – who have applied it to themselves. The New English Bible gives a better impression of the seriousness of the charge: 'The men who have made trouble all over the world have now come here . . . They all flout the Emperor's laws, and assert that there is a rival king, Jesus.' Paul, in fact, was careful to inculcate respect for imperial law and order, for which he himself had good reason to be grateful on several occasions. But

[23] In the Froehner collection; Froehner's inventory simply calls it a 'marble slab sent from Nazareth in 1878'. I have discussed it more fully in my *New Testament History* (Oliphants, London, 1971), pp. 285 ff.

[24] Cf. Acts 25. 19.

it could not be denied that he proclaimed the lordship of one who had been executed by sentence of a Roman court on a charge of claiming to be king of the Jews. Moreover, the Zealot movement was particularly active in Judaea during the principate of Claudius, and it could not be contained within the frontiers of its home province. A militant messianism was working like a ferment in Jewish communities elsewhere in the world, and the authorities were not likely to draw a distinction between it and the 'messianism' of the Christian missionaries. We have already mentioned Claudius's expulsion of the Jews from Rome because of riots in which, somehow or other, the name of Christ appears to have been mixed up.

Another piece of evidence has been preserved which some have interpreted as indicating that Claudius was concerned about the disturbances caused by the spread of Christianity throughout the Empire. This is a letter sent by him to the people of Alexandria in A.D. 41; a papyrus copy of it was acquired by the British Museum in 1921.[25] Not long before there had been violent and sanguinary riots in Alexandria, between the Greek and Jewish elements in the city's population. On his accession to the imperial power Claudius wrote to them urging them to keep the peace and exhibit mutual forbearance. Then, in an admonition intended for the Jewish community, he adds:

> Do not bring in or invite Jews who sail to Alexandria from Syria or from other parts of Egypt; this will make me suspect you the more, and I will impose severe penalties on them for fomenting a general plague throughout the whole world.

Who were these immigrant Jews? From the way in which Claudius describes them, some readers have surmised that they were Jewish Christians, possibly the first Christian missionaries to Alexandria. But the reference is more probably to Jews from other parts of Egypt and from Syria (here including Judaea) whom the Alexandrian Jews invited to join them so as to increase their strength in the event of further attacks on them by their Gentile neighbours in the city. We know that, when news arrived of the death of Claudius's predecessor Gaius, the Jews of Alexandria armed themselves in readiness for trouble of this kind.

[25] CPI ii. 153.

Even so, Jewish Christian influence in Alexandria was probably beginning to spread at this time. Only a few years had elapsed since the stoning of Stephen and the consequent dispersion of Hellenistic Jewish Christians who had until then been members of the Jerusalem church. Those who were dispersed went in all directions, taking the Christian message with them. We have explicit information about those who travelled through Syria and Phoenicia as far as Antioch (Acts 8. 4; 11. 19 ff.); it is certain that some made their way to Egypt and Cyrenaica. But their contacts with the Jewish communities of those parts were likely to cause trouble, and if Claudius got to know about them he would certainly include them under the ban which he imposed on Jewish immigrants, and he would include their teaching in his description of Jewish messianism in general as a 'plague' infesting the whole world.[26] The situation in Alexandria was already so tense that Claudius did not wish to permit any development which might lead to fresh rioting. Hence his severe language. But Christianity took root in Alexandria none the less. Some ten years later we read of a learned Alexandrian Jew named Apollos who visited Ephesus and Corinth and confounded the teachers in the synagogues there by the power of his arguments that Jesus was the true Messiah (Acts 18. 24–28).

More Inscriptional Evidence

When Paul and Barnabas visited Lystra in the course of their first missionary journey in Asia Minor, a lame man was cured with such miraculous suddenness that the local populace came to the conclusion that their city was being favoured with a visit from two of the chief gods whom they worshipped. So, says Luke, 'Barnabas they called Zeus, and Paul, because he was the chief speaker, they called Hermes' (Acts 14. 11).

Zeus was the father of gods and men, while Hermes was his herald. The older English versions latinise the names of the two gods, rendering them Jupiter and Mercury. Paul and Barnabas did not at first grasp what the populace meant, because they spoke in their own vernacular, 'the speech of Lycaonia'.

[26] Cf. Acts 24. 5, where Paul is accused before Felix of being 'a perfect plague, an agitator among all the Jews throughout the world, and a ringleader of the sect of the Nazarenes' (c. A.D. 57).

These two gods had a traditional association with that region of Asia Minor; on one occasion, for example, they had visited a neighbouring district incognito and been hospitably entertained by a poor and aged couple, Philemon and Baucis. The story is best known from the account given by the Roman poet Ovid in his *Metamorphoses*.[27] But archaeology has also had something to say on this subject.

In 1910 Sir William Calder found evidence of the association of Zeus and Hermes in the worship of the people around Lystra when he deciphered an inscription near that city which recorded the dedication to Zeus of a statue of Hermes by men with Lycaonian names. On another visit to the same district sixteen years later, in the company of Professor W. H. Buckler, he came upon a stone altar dedicated to the 'Hearer of Prayer' (that is Zeus) and Hermes.[28] It was natural, therefore, that when the men of Lystra fancied that their two visitors were gods, they should identify them with Zeus and Hermes.

In the narrative of Acts the city of Derbe is closely associated with Lystra. Derbe, we are told by an ancient lexicographer, is a Lycaonian name meaning 'juniper'; the city was so called because of the abundance of juniper bushes there.

The site of Derbe remained unknown until 1956 although Sir William Ramsay and others had made tentative suggestions about its location. But in 1956 Mr. Michael Ballance discovered a dedicatory inscription set up by the council and people of Derbe in A.D. 157. The inscription was found at the mound of Kerti Hüyük, which lies some thirteen miles N.N.E. of the modern town of Laranda, in circumstances which made it practically certain that Kerti Hüyük marks the site of the ancient Derbe.[29] The tentative suggestions previously made

---

[27] Ovid, *Metamorphoses* viii. 626 ff.

[28] Cf. W. M. Calder, 'A Cult of the Homonades', *Classical Review* 24 (1910), pp. 76 ff.; 'Christians and Pagans in the Graeco-Roman Levant', *Classical Review* 38 (1924), p. 29, n. 1; 'A Test: Acts 14. 12', *Expository Times* 37 (1925–26), p. 528.

[29] Mr. Ballance later proposed Devri Sehri, $2\frac{1}{2}$ miles S.S.E. of Kerti Hüyük, as the site. See M. Ballance, 'The Site of Derbe: A New Inscription', *Anatolian Studies* 7 (1957), pp. 147 ff.; 'Derbe and Faustinopolis', *Anatolian Studies* 14 (1964), pp. 139 f.; B. Van Elderen, 'Some Archaeological Observations on Paul's First Missionary Journey' in *Apostolic History and the Gospel*, ed. W. W. Gasque and R. P. Martin (Paternoster Press, 1970), pp. 156 ff.

located Derbe some twenty-five miles too far to the west; actually it lies sixty miles east of Lystra.

Our English versions have generally translated Acts 14. 20 in such a way as to make Paul and Barnabas reach Derbe the day after they left Lystra; it now appears more probable that we should translate: 'next day he set out with Barnabas for Derbe'. Archaeological discoveries which help towards the more accurate interpretation of Scripture are as important as those which confirm its statements.

Reference has been made above to Paul's arrival in Corinth in A.D. 50. Luke tells us that he visited the synagogue, and argued there sabbath by sabbath, contending that Jesus was the Messiah. Early in the present century the remains of an inscription over a Corinthian doorway were published: the inscription when complete had evidently read 'Synagogue of the Hebrews'.[30] From the character of the writing it is inferred that this inscription was in position in Paul's day; it is well within the bounds of possibility that it stood over the doorway through which Paul went in and out so often, until the day when he was told that the hospitality of the synagogue was no longer available to him.

In 1929 a first-century marble slab was uncovered at Corinth by an American archaeological expedition; it bore the Latin inscription: 'Erastus, in consideration of his appointment as curator of buildings, laid this pavement at his own expense.' It is inevitable that we should recall Paul's friend Erastus, city treasurer of Corinth, from whom he sends greetings to his readers in Romans 16. 23. It is not at all unlikely that the Erastus who donated the pavement was identical with the Erastus who is mentioned by Paul.[31]

Another inscription from ancient Corinth mentions the *makellon* or meat-market to which Paul refers in 1 Corinthians 10. 25 ('shambles' in the Authorized Version).[32] The raised platform or 'tribunal' from which Gallio, proconsul of Achaia, dismissed the case against Paul which was brought before him (Acts 18. 12–17) still stands among the ruins of Roman Corinth, near the centre of the Agora.

[30] Cf. A. Deissmann, *Light from the Ancient East*, p. 16.
[31] Cf. H. J. Cadbury, 'Erastus of Corinth', *Journal of Biblical Literature* 50 (1931), pp. 42 ff.
[32] Cf. H. J. Cadbury, 'The Macellum of Corinth', *Journal of Biblical Literature* 53 (1934), pp. 134 ff.

In Acts 17. 6 Luke uses a word for the city magistrates of Thessalonica which is not known in Greek literature. It is the word *politarchs*, translated 'city authorities' in the Revised Standard Version. But although this word is not found in any classical author, it has been identified in some nineteen inscriptions, all in Macedonia, ranging from the second century B.C. to the third century A.D. It was evidently a designation for the chief magistrates of Macedonian cities, including Thessalonica. Indeed, the politarchs of Thessalonica are mentioned in five out of these nineteen inscriptions; it had five politarchs at the beginning of the first century A.D., and six in the second century.[33] This illustrates one of the most impressive features of Luke's detailed accuracy—his ability to use the right technical title for the right official in one place after another throughout the provinces of the Roman Empire.

Ephesus is another place where inscriptional evidence throws light on the New Testament narrative. 'What man is there', asked the town clerk of Ephesus, 'who does not know that the city of the Ephesians is temple keeper of the great Artemis, and of the sacred stone that fell from the sky?' (Acts 19. 35). When he called the city 'temple keeper' of the great goddess, the Greek term he used was *neōkoros*, an honorific title which is accorded to the city in an inscription. It referred to the fact that Ephesus was the place where Artemis had her great temple, one of the seven wonders of the ancient world; originally the term had had the humbler connotation of 'temple *sweeper*', but it had risen in the world! The chief silversmith's claim that 'all Asia and the world' worshipped the Ephesian goddess is borne out by evidence of thirty-three places throughout the ancient world where there were shrines in her honour. The interest which the guild of silversmiths took in her cult is illustrated by an inscription of A.D. 103–4, in Greek and Latin, found in the theatre of Ephesus, recording how a Roman official, Gaius Vibius Salutaris, presented a silver image of the goddess to be set up in the theatre during a full meeting of the city assembly, or *ecclesia*.[34] It was in this theatre that the riotous

[33] Cf. E. D. Burton, 'The Politarchs', *American Journal of Theology* 2 (1898), pp. 598 ff.
[34] Cf. Deissmann, *Light from the Ancient East*, pp. 112 f.

assembly of Acts 19. 29 ff. was staged; its excavation revealed it to be capable of holding 25,000 persons.

During Paul's last visit to Jerusalem, a riot arose in the temple because the rumour got around that he had polluted the sacred precincts by taking Gentiles into them (Acts 21. 27 ff.). Gentiles might enter the outer court, which was therefore called the Court of the Gentiles; but they might not penetrate farther on pain of death. So anxious were the Roman authorities to conciliate the religious susceptibilities of the Jews that they even sanctioned the execution of Roman citizens for this offence. That none might plead ignorance of the rule, notices in Greek and Latin were fastened to the barrier separating the outer from the inner courts, warning Gentiles that death was the penalty for trespass.[35] One of these Greek inscriptions, found at Jerusalem in 1871 by C. S. Clermont-Ganneau, a French archaeologist, is now housed in the Turkish State Museum, Istanbul, and reads as follows:

No foreigner may enter within the barrier which surrounds the sanctuary and its precincts. Any one who is caught doing so will be personally responsible for his ensuing death.[36]

Another, but imperfect copy, was found over sixty years later; it is in the Rockefeller Museum in Jerusalem.[37]

Such archaeological remains do not belong to the heart of the New Testament story, but they help to fill out the context within which that story can be better appreciated.

[35] Cf. Josephus, *War* v. 193; *Antiquities* xv. 417. See p. 45.
[36] Cf. Deissmann, *Light from the Ancient East*, pp. 79 ff.
[37] Cf. J. H. Iliffe, 'The *Thanatos* Inscription from Herod's Temple: Fragments of a Second Copy', *Quarterly of Department of Antiquities in Palestine* 6 (1938), pp. 1 ff. Both copies appear to have been set up during Herod's reign (*c.* 11–10 B.C.).

Epilogue

I REMEMBER an occasion when I addressed a Rotary club on the discovery and significance of the documents from Nag Hammadi, mentioned at the beginning of Chapter 7 of this volume. During the period of questions and discussion which followed my talk, one elderly member of the audience asked more than once, in a tone of perplexity and suspicion, regarding the scholars concerned with the study and publication of those texts: 'But what are they trying to *prove*?' I fear I did not succeed in persuading him that they were not trying to 'prove' anything. The texts had been discovered accidentally, and the scholars in question were concerned simply to make them generally accessible and to assess their bearing on the history of early Christian thought and life.

But the question brought it home to me that the motivation of scholarship may be imperfectly understood by people whose interests lie elsewhere and that the ideal of the pursuit of truth for its own sake is not so self-evident to others as it is to those who are dedicated to it. It may be, then, that some readers of this book will ask what the author is trying to *prove*. Let them be assured that he is not trying to 'prove' anything; he is concerned to give an account of references to Jesus and Christian origins, factual or fictitious, outside the New Testament. He is certainly not concerned to establish the historicity of Jesus or the trustworthiness of the received account of Christian origins on such data as these: such an exercise would be based on the study of the primary sources, the New Testament writings themselves. And the treatment of the New Testament writings as primary sources is due to nothing in the nature of dogmatic preference. No body of literature, we said in our introduction, has been subjected to such intensive critical analysis as the New Testament writings, and the methods of criticism which confirm the historical inferiority of the apocryphal Gospels and related material are the methods which confirm the superiority of the New Testament writings.

Much of the material in the foregoing chapters illustrates the way in which legend gathers around certain historical figures. A parallel case is that of Alexander the Great, around whose name a cycle of romantic stories took shape from the early third century A.D. to the fifteenth century, from Britain to Malaya. This cycle bears but little relation to the historical facts of Alexander's career, but its existence in no way impairs the credibility of the historical facts; rather it testifies to the exceptional impact which the memory of Alexander and his exploits made throughout Europe and Asia. Similarly the proliferation of legends about Jesus, in the apocryphal Gospels and elsewhere, in no way impairs the historical validity of his life and ministry; rather it bears witness to the increasing impact of his person and achievement both within Christendom and beyond its frontiers, even among people who had no experience of his redeeming grace.

Bibliography

INTRODUCTION AND CHAPTER I

Betz, O., *What do we know about Jesus?* (S.C.M., 1968)
Bruce, F. F., *The New Testament Documents: Are They Reliable?* (I.V.P., 5th edition, London, 1960)
Dodd, C. H., *History and the Gospel* (James Nisbet & Co., 1938; Hodder & Stoughton, 1964)
Dodd, C. H., *The Founder of Christianity* (Collins, 1972)
Manson, T. W., *The Servant Messiah* (C.U.P., 1953)

CHAPTERS II AND III

Josephus, *The Jewish War*, translated by G. A. Williamson (Penguin, 1959)
Glatzer, N. H. (ed.), *Jerusalem and Rome. The Writings of Josephus* (Collins, 1966)
Jack, J. W., *The Historic Christ* (J. Clarke, London, 1933)
Montefiore, H. W., *Josephus and the New Testament* (Mowbrays, 1962)
Williamson, G. A., *The World of Josephus* (Secker & Warburg, 1964)

CHAPTER IV

Herford, R. T., *Christianity in Talmud and Midrash* (Williams & Norgate, 1903; new ed. Gregg International, 1972)
Klausner, J., *Jesus of Nazareth* (Collier-Macmillan, 1929)

CHAPTER V

Bruce, F. F., *Second Thoughts on the Dead Sea Scrolls* (3rd edition, Paternoster Press, 1966)
Russell, D. S., *The Jews from Alexander to Herod* (O.U.P., 1967)
Vermes, G., *The Dead Sea Scrolls in English* (Penguin, 1962)

CHAPTERS VI, VII AND VIII

Bell, H. I., and Skeat, T. C. (ed.), *Fragments of an Unknown Gospel and Other Early Christian Papyri* (Brit. Mus., 1935)

Doresse, J., *The Secret Books of the Egyptian Gnostics* (Hollis & Carter, 1960)

Finegan, J., *Hidden Records of the Life of Jesus* (Pilgrim Press, Philadelphia, 1969)

Grant, R. M., and Freedman, D. N. (ed.), *Secret Sayings of Jesus* (Collins, 1960)

Schneemelcher, W. (ed.), *New Testament Apocrypha*, Eng. tr. edited by R. McL. Wilson, Vol. I, *Gospels and Related Writings* (Lutterworth Press, 1963)

Jeremias, J., *Unknown Sayings of Jesus* (S.P.C.K., 3rd edition, 1964)

CHAPTERS IX AND X

Arberry, A. J., *The Koran Interpreted* (O.U.P., 1955)

Dawood, N. J. (tr.), *The Koran* (Penguin, 1956)

Dunkerley, R., *Beyond the Gospels* (Penguin, 1957)

Robson, J., *Christ in Islam* (John Murray, London, 1929)

Watt, W. M., *Islamic Revelation in the Modern World* (Edinburgh U.P., 1969)

CHAPTER XI

Finegan, J., *The Archaeology of the New Testament* (Princeton U.P., 1969)

Harrison, R. K., *Archaeology of the New Testament* (E.U.P., 1964)

Millard, A. R. (ed.), *Documents of New Testament Times* (I.V.P., London, forthcoming)

Index

INDEX